S. A. W Jewett

Livingston in Africa

His explorations and missionary labors

S. A. W Jewett

Livingston in Africa
His explorations and missionary labors

ISBN/EAN: 9783744758321

Printed in Europe, USA, Canada, Australia, Japan

Cover: Foto ©Andreas Hilbeck / pixelio.de

More available books at **www.hansebooks.com**

Livingstone in Africa:

HIS

Explorations and Missionary Labors.

BY

REV. S. A. W. JEWETT.

With Illustrations.

CINCINNATI:

HITCHCOCK & WALDEN.

NEW YORK:

CARLTON & LANAHAN.

PREFATORY NOTE.

THE pretensions of this little volume are not at all ambitious. Its aim is simply to recite the missionary travels of Rev. David Livingstone, LL. D., accomplished in South Africa, between the years 1840 and 1856, in smaller compass than the large narrative written by himself. The task was entered upon in the hope of bringing the noble work of that eminent Christian philanthropist to the attention of a class of readers who, for various reasons, may pass by the larger volume. All the material facts and incidents essential to a just idea of the country, the habits and character of the people, and the hardships and toil of the great traveler will be found here. In describing the same events and objects, similarity of language must often occur. But where that may most appear, complete reconstruction of style has been found necessary in order to secure uniformity and brevity.

S. A. W. J.

CHICAGO, *February* 20, 1868.

CONTENTS.

————◇————

CHAPTER I.

CHAPTER II.

CHAPTER III.

CHAPTER IV.

5

ILLUSTRATIONS.

LIVINGSTONE IN AFRICA.

CHAPTER I.

BEFORE entering directly upon our pleasant task, let us glance a moment at the boyhood of that noble man whose footsteps we propose to trace across the African continent. That glance, though it be a brief one, will no doubt inspire us with respect and love for him; and perhaps awaken in our minds a deeper sympathy with his life. of unselfish toil.

His early home was in a little manufacturing village near Glasgow, Scotland. His father was a small tea-dealer—a man of devoted and consistent piety. Though he never became rich, yet, "by his kindliness of manner and winning ways, he made the heart-strings of his children

twine around him as firmly as if he had possessed, and could have bestowed upon them every
worldly advantage." These words just quoted
are from Dr. Livingstone himself, as the reader
may have guessed. And in these which follow,
he mentions his mother, and tells how his education began.

"The earliest recollection of my mother re-
calls a picture so often seen among the Scottish
poor—that of the anxious housewife striving to
make both ends meet. At the age of ten I was
put into the factory as a 'piecer,' to aid by my
earnings in lessening her anxiety. With a part
of my first week's wages I purchased Ruddi-
man's 'Rudiments of Latin,' and pursued the
study of that language for many years afterward
with unabated ardor, at an evening school which
met between the hours of eight and ten. The
dictionary part of my labors was followed up till
twelve o'clock, or later, if my mother did not
interfere by jumping up and snatching the books
out of my hands. I had to be back in the factory by six in the morning, and continue my
work, with intervals for breakfast and dinner, till
eight o'clock at night. I read in this way many
of the classical authors, and knew Virgil and
Horace better at sixteen than I do now."

At the age of nineteen young Livingstone was

promoted to the work of cotton-spinning. So intense was his love of study that he kept it up in the factory amid the noise of the machinery. His book was placed on a part of the spinning-jenny, where he could catch a sentence at a time as he passed back and forth at his work. In this manner he acquired a discipline of mind which enabled him in after life to write with ease when surrounded by the songs, and dancing of savages. And by this severe labor he gained a hardiness of body which fitted him to endure the excessive toil, and exposure of his long years of missionary travel. By work in the factory during the Summer months he provided means of self-support while in Winter time attending Divinity lectures, and Greek and medical classes in Glasgow.

Does the life of this young man seem to any of my readers a hard and irksome lot? Would you then like to know what he thought of it in his later years? Was he ashamed of the hard and lowly work of his boyhood? His own words shall answer. When his name had become famous throughout the world, and the learned and great delighted to do him honor, he did not hide the fact that his education was earned by the labor of his own hands. He nobly said, "Looking back now on that life of toil, I can but feel

thankful that it formed such a material part of
my early education, and were it possible I should
like to begin life over again in the same lowly
style, and to pass through the same hardy train-
ing. . . . . Time and travel have not ef-
faced the feelings of respect I imbibed for the
humble inhabitants of my native village."

In all this earnest work young Livingstone
had an ardent desire to fit himself for future use-
fulness. Having become a Christian by yielding
his heart to Christ, the glowing love to God and
man which this new experience kindled, led him
to form the purpose of giving his life to the
work of planting Christianity in China. He
hoped to gain access to the people of that vast
empire by means of the healing art ; and with
that object in view he set himself to the task of
acquiring a medical education. But when he
had finished his studies and received his diploma
constituting him a member of the " Faculty of
Physicians and Surgeons," a new obstacle to the
execution of his original plan arose. The opium
war between England and China was raging, and
this made it inexpedient to begin his fondly
cherished enterprise. Just at this time a new
and inviting field of labor was opened up in
South Africa, by the labors of Rev. Robert
Moffat, his father-in-law. There being no pros-

pect of an early peace in China, he with some reluctance yielded to the advice of friends, and offered himself to the London Missionary Society for their work in Africa; and after pursuing a more extensive course of theological study, he sailed, in 1840, for the African continent, under the auspices of that society. A voyage of three months brought him to Cape Town. Here he spent but a short time, and then sailing along the coast to Algoa Bay, he started at once for the interior.

A look at the map of South Africa will refresh the mind of the reader as to the locality of these places, and help him to form a better and more vivid conception of that vast field of labor where our missionary traveler and his family spent sixteen years of toil and exposure among savage men—that he might teach them the "glorious Gospel of Christ," and prepare the way for the introduction of a Christian civilization to all that immense country. The journey from Algoa Bay northward to Kuruman or Lattakoo—a distance of seven hundred miles—was made in wagons drawn by oxen. This place is a central mission station for the surrounding country. Resting here only long enough to recruit the tired oxen, Livingstone proceeded still farther north, in company with another missionary, to the country of the Bakwains. Their chief was found, with his people, at Shokuane. The town, or village, was composed of numerous circles of huts gathered around a large one in the center, which was that of the principal chief, Sechele. The government and constitution of these native tribes is patriarchal. Each man is the chief of his own children; and the more numerous his family, the greater will be his importance in the tribe. Hence, children are always treated kindly, and are thought the greatest of blessings. As they grow up the children build their huts in a circle around that of their father. Near the center of the circle there is a fireplace; and this, with a little space close around it, is called a " Kotla." Here the families eat and work, and at the evening hour sit together around the fireplace and talk over the news of the day. Sometimes a poor man joins the Kotla of a rich one, and so becomes his child. The huts in the circle immediately around the Kotla of the chief are occupied by his wives and blood relations. Around those of each under chief there are a number of Kotlas with their circles. And the whole collection of circles gathered around the Kotla of the principal chief constitutes the town.

There are several Bechuana tribes. Each one of them is named for some animal. And each tribe has a superstitious fear of the animal for which it is named ; and the flesh of that animal they never eat. The name Bechuana, or Bakwain, means "They of the alligator;" Bakatla, "They of the monkey;" Batlapi, "They of the fish." This custom of using the personal pronoun in the names of tribes prevails very extensively in Africa. They use the word "bina" in connection with this manner of naming themselves. Thus, if you want to know what tribe one belongs to, you ask, "What do you dance?" He replies, "The alligator," "The monkey," or, "The fish." These singular customs have been thought an indication that in earlier times they practiced the worship of animals, like the ancient Egyptians, and that dancing formed a part of that old worship.

Livingstone attached himself to the tribe of the Bakwains ; and after a few months spent in journeys and preparation—during which time he returned once to Kuruman—he began a settlement at Lepelole, about fifteen miles south of Shokuane. He dug a canal to conduct water to the gardens from a full and flowing river, which afterward became dry. While here he excluded himself from all society, except that of the natives, for the purpose of acquiring more perfect knowledge of their habits of thinking, their customs, laws, and language. This proved of very great advantage to him in his subsequent intercourse with them.

After getting the arrangements for the settlement well advanced, he made a journey northward to the Bakao Mountains, accompanied by several natives. These mountains had been visited before, by a trader, who perished with his whole party. In passing around the northern part of these basaltic hills, near Letloche, Livingstone was within ten days' journey of the Zonga, which flows into Lake Ngami—pronounced Ingami, the initial I soft as possible.

Had discovery been his chief object, he might have discovered the lake at this time—1842. The oxen being sick, much of this journey had to be performed on foot. The natives did not know that Livingstone understood their language, and he one day overheard them talking of his appearance and power of enduring fatigue. " He is not strong," they said. " He is quite slim, and only seems stout because he puts himself into those bags "—meaning his pantaloons—"he will soon give out." This stirred the Highland blood of our traveler so that he kept them at the top of their speed for several days, till he heard them express better opinions of his power as a pedestrian.

Returning to Kuruman for the purpose of removing his luggage to the proposed settlement, Livingstone was followed with the discouraging news that his friends the Bakwains had been driven from that part of the country by the Barolongs. One of those outbreaks of war for the possession of cattle, which occur from time to time among these tribes, had burst forth, and destroyed all prospect of establishing a mission station at Lepelole, or Litubaruba, for the present. This made it necessary to look up some new locality.

But another matter first demanded attention. Some of the Bamangwato people having accompanied our missionary on his late return from the North, he was obliged to make a journey to the residence of their chief, Sekomi, to restore them and their goods to him. On this journey he for the first time mounted an ox, and rode several hundred miles in that manner. Upon his return the beautiful valley of Mabotsa was selected for the missionary station. And to this place he removed in 1843.

While living here he had an encounter with a lion, in which he was handled rather roughly, although he came off the conqueror at last. The people of the village—the Bakatla—were greatly troubled by the lions, which leaped into their

2

cattle pens and destroyed their cows.   The herds
were, too, sometimes attacked in open day.   This
being quite unusual, the people believed themselves bewitched.   They were given, they said,
"into the power of the lions by a neighboring
tribe."   Such are the habits of this animal, that
if one from a troop of lions is killed his comrades profit by the hint, and quit, for a time, that
part of the country.   The people of the village
went out once to attack the animals, but being
cowardly, they came back without killing one.
So when the herds were next attacked Livingstone went out with the men to inspire them
with courage, and aid them in getting rid of the
annoyance.   The rest of the story he shall give
you in his own words.

"We found the lions on a small hill, about a
quarter of a mile in length, and covered with
trees.   A circle of men was formed round it, and
they gradually closed up, ascending pretty near
to each other.   Being down below, on the plain,
with a native schoolmaster named Mebalwe, a
most excellent man, I saw one of the lions sitting
on a piece of rock within the now closed circle
of men.   Mebalwe fired at him before I could,
and the ball struck the rock on which the animal was sitting.   He bit at the spot struck, as a
dog does at a stick or stone thrown at him;

then leaping away, broke through the opening circle and escaped unhurt. The men were afraid to attack him, perhaps on account of their belief in witchcraft. When the circle was re-formed, we saw two other lions in it, but we were afraid to fire, lest we should strike the men, and they allowed the beasts to burst through also. If the Bakatla had acted according to the custom of the country, they would have speared the lions in their attempt to get out. Seeing we could not get them to kill one of the lions, we bent our footsteps toward the village. In going round the end of the hill, however, I saw one of the beasts sitting on a piece of rock as before, but this time he had a little bush in front.

"Being about thirty yards off, I took a good aim at his body through the bush, and fired both barrels into it. The men then called out, 'He is shot, he is shot.' Others cried, 'He has been shot by another man, too; let us go to him!' I did not see any one else shoot at him, but I saw the lion's tail erected in anger behind the bush, and turning to the people, said, 'Stop a little till I load again.' When in the act of ramming down the bullets I heard a shout. Starting and looking half round, I saw the lion just in the act of springing upon me. I was upon a little hight. He caught my shoulder as he sprang, and we both came to the ground below together. Growling horribly close to my ear, he shook me as a terrier dog does a rat. The shock produced a stupor similar to that which seems to be felt by a mouse after the first shake of the cat. It caused a sort of dreaminess, in which there was no sense of pain, nor feeling of terror, though quite conscious of all that was happening. It was like what patients partially under the influence of chloroform describe, who see all the operation, but feel not the knife.

"This singular condition was not the result of any mental process. The shake annihilated fear, and allowed no sense of horror in looking round at the beast. This peculiar state is probably produced in all animals killed by the carnivora; and if so, is a merciful provision by our benevolent Creator for lessening the pain of death. Turning round to relieve myself of the weight, as he had one paw on the back of my head, I saw his eyes directed to Mebalwe, who was trying to shoot him at a distance of ten or fifteen yards. His gun, a flint one, missed fire in both barrels. The lion immediately left me, and attacking Mebalwe, bit his thigh. Another man, whose life I had saved before, after he had been tossed by a buffalo, attempted to spear the lion while he was biting Mebalwe. He left Mebalwe and caught

THE MISSIONARY'S ESCAPE FROM THE LION.

this man by the shoulder, but at that moment the bullets he had received took effect, and he fell down dead. The whole was the work of a few moments, and must have been his paroxysms of dying rage."

Livingstone's victory over the king of beasts was rather dearly bought. He came out of the fight with the bone of his arm crushed to splinters by the jaws of the lion, and eleven flesh wounds from his teeth in the upper part of it. The Bakatla declared him the largest lion they had ever seen ; and the next day they built a huge bonfire over the carcass to take the charm of witchcraft out of him.

The wound inflicted by the lion's tooth is much like that caused by a gunshot. It is usually followed by much discharge, and sloughing off of the flesh ; and it is a curious fact that ever afterward pains are felt in the wounded part on the return of the same period of the year. Mebalwe suffered in this way from the bite in his thigh ; and the wound of the man who was bitten in the shoulder actually burst forth afresh on the same month of the following year. But fortunately our hero-missionary fared better than his comrades. He wore in the affray a tartan jacket ; and the woolen through which the teeth passed in piercing his flesh seems to have wiped

the virus from them. And thus he escaped with
only the inconvenience of a false joint in his
limb.

Before going any further in our travels, let me
give my readers a brief sketch of the history and
character of Sechele, the chief of the Bakwains,
with whom our missionary lived for several
years. By Doctor Livingstone's account of him
he was a remarkable man, and very intelligent.
His great-grandfather, Mochoasele, was a great
traveler, and was the first who told the Bakwains
of the existence of white men. In the lifetime
of Sechele's father two white travelers passed
through the country of this tribe, and descending the river Limpopo, they, with all their party,
died of fever. These travelers are supposed to
have been Doctor Cowan and Captain Donovan,
who were in Africa in 1808, and were reported
to have been killed by the Bangwaketse. This
statement was given to Livingstone by a son of
the chief at whose village they died. He said
he remembered when a boy having eaten part of
one of their horses, which tasted like the flesh
of a zebra.

When Sechele was only a boy, his father, who
was also named Mochoasele, was killed by his
own people, in punishment for taking to himself
the wives of some of his rich under chiefs. The

children of the murdered chief were spared; and
their friends soon sought the aid of Sebituane,
the chief of the Makalolo, to restore them to
their rights in the chieftainship. Sebituane, with
his people, surrounded the town of the Bakwains
by night; and when the day began to dawn his
herald proclaimed in a loud voice that he had
come to revenge the death of Mochoasele. This
was followed by a terrific noise, caused by Sebituane's men beating loudly upon their shields all
around the town. The panic-stricken Bakwains
rushed from their huts like a crowd from a burning theater, while their enemies used their javelins upon them with great dexterity and effect.

Orders had been given the men by Sebituane
to spare the sons of the chief; but Sechele being
met by one of them, received a blow from a club
on the head, which made him insensible. The
attack ended in the death of the usurper, and the
establishment of Sechele in the chieftainship;
and he became warmly attached to Sebituane,
who had so befriended him in his adversity.

It is the custom with these African tribes for
the chief to bind his under chiefs to himself and
his government by marrying their daughters. So
Sechele married the daughters of three of his
under chiefs. They are all very fond of being
known as relatives of some great man. If, when

traveling, you meet a party of strangers, and the relationship of the head man is not at once proclaimed by his attendants, you hear him whisper, "Tell him who I am ;" and after counting a part of his genealogical tree on their fingers, the performance closes with the important statement that the head man of the party is half-cousin to some noted chief.

On the occasion when Livingstone made his first attempt to hold a public religious service among the Bakwains, Sechele remarked that it was the custom of his nation when any new subject was brought before them to ask questions upon it, and he begged permission to do so in this case. Our missionary having expressed his readiness to answer questions, Sechele asked him if his forefathers knew of a future judgment. He was answered in the affirmative, and a description given him, from the Bible, of the "great white throne, and Him who shall sit on it, from whose face the heaven and earth shall flee away," when he said, "You startle me; these words make all my bones to shake—I have no strength in me. But my forefathers were living at the same time yours were, and how is it that they did not send them word about these terrible things sooner? They all passed away into darkness without knowing whither they were going."

This difficulty was met by explaining the gradual spread of knowledge from the South, by the means of ships, and the want of access from the North in former times.

Soon as the opportunity was given him, Sechele applied himself with great diligence to the task of learning to read. He learned the alphabet on the first day, and gave up his hunting, of which he was very fond, that he might give more time to study. Having acquired the art of reading, he was fond of showing his accomplishment, and pressed Doctor Livingstone, whenever he came into the town, to hear him read from the Bible. Among the writers of the inspired Volume Isaiah was his particular favorite. He used to say, " He was a fine man, that Isaiah; he knew how to speak."

One day, upon seeing the anxiety of our missionary that his people should believe the words of Jesus, he said, " Do you imagine these people will ever believe by your merely talking to them? I can make them do nothing except by thrashing them; and if you like I shall call my head men, and with our litupa—whips of rhinoceros hide— we will soon make them all believe together." He would not condescend to ask the opinion of his subjects on any other matter, and he was surprised that the missionary should be content with merely persuading them to become Christians. Having himself embraced Christianity, and hoping to induce others to do so, he asked Livingstone to begin family worship with him in his house. He then conducted it himself, and being a master of his own language, it was a pleasant surprise to the missionary to hear in how simple and beautiful a style he offered prayer. He felt keenly the difficulties in which his heathen practices involved him. By his study of the Bible he found that Christianity forbids polygamy ; and he could not get rid of his superfluous wives without seeming to be ungrateful to their parents and families, who had stood by him and helped him in the adversity of his early life. He often said to our missionary, " O, I wish you had come to this country before I became entangled in the meshes of our customs."

Seeing the difficulty of the case, and feeling compassion for the women, Livingstone did not wish him to be in haste to make a full and public profession of Christianity by baptism, and by putting away all but one of his wives. Some of them, too, were among the best scholars in the mission school, and his principal wife seemed less likely than almost any other person in the tribe to become any thing else than a greasy disciple of heathenism. Again and again was Sechele

compelled to send her out of Church to put on her
gown ; and out she would go, with her pouting
lips and whole manner expressing her deep disgust at his new-fangled notions. She did, however, very greatly improve afterward. When, after
a consistent profession of about three years, he
applied for baptism, Livingstone asked him how,
having the Bible in his hand, and able to read it,
he himself thought he ought to act. He at once
went home, gave each of his extra wives new
clothing, and the goods they had been keeping
for him in their huts, and sent them to their parents with the statement that he found no fault
with them, but parted with them that he might
obey God.

Large numbers came to witness the ceremony
when he and his children were baptized. A stupid story had been told by the enemies of Christianity that the converts were required to drink
an infusion of "dead men's brains." Some believed it, and were surprised that only water was
used in the baptismal service. Some of the old
men wept to see their father—as they called the
chief—so bewitched by the white man. And
now our missionary had to meet a new opposition. Though himself and family were still
treated with respectful kindness, yet all the
friends of the divorced wives became enemies of

religion.   They talked to Sechele in a manner
which, before his conversion, would have cost them
their lives.   The Church and school were forsaken
by nearly all except the chief and his family.

The protracted and distressing droughts which
they suffered about this time had something to
do with this opposition ; for the Bakwains thought
the destitution of rain was in some way connected with the presence among them of " God's
word," and the Christian teacher.   They had
been visited the first year that Livingstone settled among them, at Chonuane, with one of those
severe droughts which occasionally occur in the
most favored districts of Africa.   By his advice
the tribe removed forty miles distant, to the river
Kolobeng.

Here our missionary erected the third house,
which he built with his own hands.   In exchange
for his labor in aiding them to build a square
house for their chief, the men of the tribe built a
dam across the river, and made a canal to water
the fields and gardens.   The plan worked finely
the first year ; but in the two following years not
ten inches of rain fell, and the river ran dry.   All
the hyenas of the country, far and near, were
unable to devour the multitude of fish which
were killed.   A huge old alligator, who had
proved a harmless neighbor, was left high and

dry in the mud. The drought continued the fourth year—very little rain falling. Needles lying for months out of doors did not rust. The leaves of native trees were shriveled. To keep the fruit trees alive they dug wells in the bed of the river, going deeper and deeper as the water receded. But all in vain. So intense was the heat that a thermometer, placed with its bulb three inches below the surface of the ground, showed the mercury standing at 132°. A certain kind of beetles, placed on the surface of the ground, ran about only a few minutes, and died from the burning heat. But the long-legged black ants were as lively and active as ever. Speaking of their tireless activity, Livingstone says: "Their organs of motion seem endowed with the same power which is ascribed by physiologists to the muscles of the human heart, by which that part of the frame never becomes fatigued, and which may be imparted to all our bodily organs in that higher sphere to which we fondly hope to rise." These tiny creatures seem to have some mysterious power of gathering moisture. In the midst of all this drought and heat, their little chambers were always moist.

This was found to be the case even in the house which was built upon a rock, many hundred feet above the bed of the river, where alone a drop of water could be found. When there was no dew they were able to moisten the burnt and dusty soil so as to make mortar for building the little galleries with which they hide their paths from the sight of birds.

The Bakwains, like the neighboring tribes, believe in the power of rain-making. It is, they think, a gift with which their rain-doctors are endowed. In procuring rain they use medicines which they think act by some mysterious charm. All medicines, they suppose, act in this way in curing diseases of the human body. Their word for cure, *alaha*, means charm. The medicines of the rain-doctor are lions' and baboons' hearts, jackals' livers, with various other parts of different animals, plants, bulbs, and roots. When the rain-doctor would charm the clouds to bring rain, he selects some particular bulbous-root, pounds it, and steeps a part, making a liquid which, when cold, he administers to a sheep. The patient dies in five minutes afterward. The remaining part of the root is burned, and the smoke ascends toward the sky. In a day or two rain comes, and all the people praise the skill of the rain-doctor and the power of his medicines. Sechele had been a famous rain-doctor, and during this long drought of which we have been speaking, the natives believed that Livingstone had bound him by some magic spell; and deputations of the old men came to him and besought him just to allow Sechele to make a few showers, saying, "The corn will die if you refuse, and we shall be scattered. Only let him make rain this once, and we shall all, men, women, and children, come to the school and sing and pray as long as you please."

An uncle of Sechele, a very sensible man, and one of influence in the tribe, said to our missionary at one time: "We like you as well as if you had been born among us; you are the only white man we can become familiar with, but we wish you to give up that everlasting preaching and praying, we can not become familiar with that at all. You see we never get rain, while those tribes who never pray as we do obtain abundance." And Livingstone says, "This was a fact; we often saw it raining on the hills ten miles off, while it would not look at us 'even with one eye.' If the Prince of the power of the air had no hand in scorching us up, I fear I often gave him credit for doing so."

Still the conduct of the people was exceedingly good during this most trying time of drought, so long continued. The men engaged in hunting, the women sold their ornaments to buy corn from their more fortunate neighbors, and the

children scoured the country to gather the numerous bulbs and roots which sustain life.

A great number of buffaloes, zebras, giraffes,
ramas, rhinoceroses, and other kinds of game
gathered about some fountains near Kolobeng.
Sixty or seventy head of this large game were
sometimes caught in a single week in the trap
called "*hopo.*" This trap is made by constructing
two hedges, so placed as to form a letter V.
But instead of coming together at the angle, the
hedges are made to form a narrow lane of about
one hundred and fifty feet in length. At the end
of this lane a pit is dug, six or eight feet deep,
and twelve or fifteen feet square. Trees are
placed along the sides of the pit, so as to hang
over the edge and prevent escape. These borders are decked with short green rushes, so as to
conceal the pitfall. The hedges are often a mile
long, and as far apart at the open end of the
hopo. By making a circle of three or four miles
around the country adjoining the opening, a tribe
can hardly fail to inclose large numbers of game.
And by closing up gradually, they are driven into
the trap. As they reach the narrow part of
it, men hidden in ambush throw javelins into
the frightened animals ; and the whole herd
rush madly forward through the lane into the
pit. Some escape by running over the backs

of others, but the greater number are entrapped.
Those which are not killed by the fall or smoth-
ered by the living mass piled above them, are
dispatched with the spear. The scene is frightful. The men are wild with excitement, and
spear the lovely creatures without mercy. Every
now and then the whole mass is made to heave
with the dying agonies of those at the bottom of
the pit. All, both rich and poor, share the game.
Meat thus obtained cured the bad effects of an
exclusive vegetable diet. Salt was found a remedy for the same difficulty. The native doctors
mixed it with their medicines when treating cases
of that kind. But Livingstone cured the disease
with salt alone.

The uncertainty of food among these people
made frequent absence from home necessary, in
order to hunt game or gather fruits and roots.
And this irregularity of life was found to be a
serious obstacle in the way of their progress in
knowledge. The experiment of missionary labor
among them was such as to show the correctness
of that growing sentiment among modern Christians, which pictures the true missionary, not as a
man going about with only a Bible in his hand,
but as one having that sacred book in one hand
and a loaf of bread in the other. We must feed
healthy feelings into the starving, in order to

3

prepare them to listen to the Gospel which we preach to them. And this is true both of the poor at home and the heathen abroad. Upon this subject Livingstone says: "My observations on this subject make me extremely desirous to promote the preparation of the raw materials of European manufactures in Africa, for by that means we may not only put a stop to the slave-trade, but introduce the negro family into the body-corporate of nations, no one member of which can suffer without the others suffering with it. Success in this, in both Eastern and Western Africa, would lead, in the course of time, to a much larger diffusion of the blessings of civilization than efforts exclusively spiritual and educational, confined to one small tribe. These, however, it would, of course, be extremely desirable to carry on at the same time at large central and healthy stations, for neither civilization nor Christianity can be promoted alone. In fact, they are inseparable."

Another influence adverse to the missionary work among the Bakwains was the nearness of the "Magaliesberg," or Boers of the Cashan Mountains. The word Boer means farmer. The Cape Colonists pass, sometimes, by that name. The Boers, generally, are a sober, industrious, and hospitable body of peasantry. Those here

spoken of are a class of men who have broken
away from English law, mainly because it makes
no distinction between the white and black man.
English law emancipated their Hottentot slaves,
and they felt themselves greatly aggrieved ; and
to escape the authority of the British Government they fled toward the interior, and formed
themselves into a republic, where, without interference from others, they can pursue " the proper
treatment of the blacks." This means with them
involuntary, unpaid labor, which is the essential
element of slavery. A part of these Boers, commanded by the late Hendrick Potgeiter, pene-
trated the interior as far as the Cashan Mountains, whence the well-known Caffre Dingaan
had just driven out a Zulu or Caffre chief, named
Mosilikatze. The Bechuana tribes of this part
of the country, glad to escape the cruel sway
of this chieftain, gave the Boers a hearty welcome. They came with the prestige of white
men and deliverers. But the poor natives soon
found they had made a sad exchange of masters,
for, as they said, " Mosilikatze was cruel to his
enemies, and kind to those he conquered; but
the Boers destroyed their enemies, and made
slaves of their friends." The native tribes are
permitted to retain a semblance of freedom, but
are forced to perform all the labor of their mas-

ters' fields, and at the same time support themselves. They build dams and canals, manure the
land, do the weeding, reaping, and building ; and
for it all they do not receive a farthing of wages.

Livingstone was himself an eye-witness of
the Boers coming to a village and demanding
twenty or thirty women to weed their gardens ;
and their demand was met by the women going
to their unpaid toil, carrying their implements
of labor on their shoulders, their own food on
their heads, and their children on their backs.
And from Mr. Potgeiter and Mr. Krieger, who
are the governors, down to the lowest among the
Boers, they make no attempt to conceal the
meanness of using unpaid toil, but justify it, and
praise their own humanity by saying, " We make
the people work for us, in consideration of allowing them to live in our country." My readers
will remember that these " people " are the natives of the country, and had it in possession
long before the Boers saw it. But this kind of
slavery only supplies the labor of the field ; and
in order to provide themselves with domestic
servants, they frequently make forays on tribes
having plenty of cattle, to capture their children
and steal the cattle. The method adopted is
this : The expedition is planned in Winter time,
when horses can be used without danger of

losing them by disease. A company of Boers, mounted on horseback, and well armed, compel some of the natives friendly to the tribe which is to be attacked, to go along with them. When they reach the village these friendly natives are arranged in front, to form a breastwork, or "shield," as they call it. The Boers then coolly fire over their heads, upon the doomed tribe; and they, being generally without fire-arms, soon fly, leaving their wives, children, and cattle a prey to their enemies. Livingstone testifies that during his residence in the interior nine such forays as this were made, and in no instance did the Boers lose a drop of blood.

The only means by which a young man in these tribes can rise to importance and respectability is to obtain cattle; hence, many of them leave home to procure work in Cape Colony. Here they build dikes and dams for the Dutch farmers, and are content if by working three or four years they can return with as many cows. On presenting one to the chief, they take rank as respectable men in the tribe.

To prevent these laborers from going to the Colony, the Boers passed a law to deprive them of the cattle their hard toil had earned, giving in justification this momentous reason: "If they want to work, let them work for us, their mas-

ters ;" and at the same time they boasted that in
their case the work would not be paid for.   I
wonder if the fire of indignation does not kindle
in the heart of my readers at the thought of such
injustice and outrage.   I think it did, a little, in
the noble-minded Livingstone.   He says, directly
in this connection, " I can never cease to be most
unfeignedly thankful that I was not born in a
land of slaves.   No one can understand the effect
of the unutterable meanness of the slave-system
on the minds of those who, but for the strange
obliquity which prevents them from feeling the
degradation, of not being gentlemen enough to
pay for services rendered, would be equal in
virtue to ourselves.   Fraud becomes as natural
to them as 'paying one's way' is to the rest of
mankind."

How heartily we, as Americans, ought to
thank God that a system involving such " *unutterable meanness* " and " degradation " has at last
been swept from our noble land !   But ought
not our cheeks to tingle with indignant shame
that the spirit of this vile system of injustice
still lingers in some hearts and some localities
among us ?

CHAPTER II.

A Glimpse of Missionary Life—Story of the Black Pot—Eating Frogs—Travel in the Desert—Water Suckers.

IN the previous chapter we have been introduced to the native Africans, with whom Livingstone lived for several years. Let us now inquire a little after his mode of living in that wild country, so far from all the conveniences of civilization. There are no shops and stores ready to supply every thing you want; there are no mechanics awaiting your command. So every thing you need for housekeeping you must manufacture yourself, from the raw material. When our missionary wanted bricks with which to build a house, he had to go to the field, chop down a tree, and saw out the planks for brick-molds. Lumber for the doors and windows he made in the same way. The three large houses which he built among the Bakwains must have cost him a vast amount of hard work. Every brick and stick had to be placed by his own right hand; for though the natives are willing to work for wages, yet it is a curious fact that they are utterly unable to place any thing square. Every thing they build is round. If you want to be respected by them you must have a large house. Livingstone, as you will remember, helped them to build a square house for their chief, at Kolobeng. So you see, besides being a doctor and preacher, he was a carpenter and builder. In order to raise food for his family, he had also to be a gardener. A native smith taught him how to weld iron, and he was indeed a jack-of-all-trades. His wife, too, was of necessity maid-of-all-work in the house.

The method of housekeeping differed somewhat from that with which we are familiar. The bread was often baked in an extempore oven, made by digging out a large hole in an ant-hill, with a slab of stone for a door. Another method sometimes employed is to build a fire on a level piece of ground, and when the soil is thoroughly heated place the dough on the hot ashes, or in a small frying-pan; then cover it with an inverted iron kettle, draw the ashes around, and build a little fire on the top. By mixing a little leaven from a former baking with the dough, and allowing it to stand an hour or two in the sun, excellent bread is made in this way.

Our missionary's family made their own butter,

candles, and soap. The independence and romance of this mode of living very much relieves its hardship. Domestic comforts are the sweeter because springing so directly from one's own skill and toil, and that of the thrifty housewife.

Take a single day as a sample of missionary life. The family rise early, because the morning is refreshing, however hot the day may be. The same is true of the evening. You may sit outdoors till midnight without fear of coughs or rheumatism. After family worship breakfast is had, between six and seven. Then the missionary opens school for all who will come—men, women, and children. School being over, at eleven he goes to his work as a gardener, smith, or carpenter. Sometimes he exchanges skilled labor with the people for unskilled work in the garden or elsewhere. Meanwhile the patient, toiling wife is employed in domestic duties. After dinner and an hour of rest she goes to her infant school, of which the young Bakwains are very fond, and to which they muster a hundred strong. Occasionally the time is given to a sewing school for girls, who like it equally well. Every operation in house or garden must be carefully superintended, and thus both the missionary and his wife are kept constantly busy, from early morning till the sun sinks in the

west.   After sunset the missionary goes into
the town, to talk with any willing to listen, upon
general subjects or religion.   On three nights
each week, after the milking of the cows is over,
and it has become dark, a public religious service
is held ; and one evening a week is devoted to
instruction on secular subjects, illustrated by pictures and specimens.

These services were sometimes varied a little
by attending the sick and prescribing for them,
or by giving food and assistance to the poor and
wretched.   Following the example of their Di-
vine Master, these benevolent disciples of Christ
sought to gain the affections of the people by
ministering to the wants of their bodies.   They
regarded the smallest act of kindness—even a
friendly word or look—as no unworthy part of
the missionary armor.   They thought the good
opinion of the most abject was worth caring for,
when it could be secured by politeness ; since
that opinion helps to form a reputation that may
be used for extending the influence of the Gospel.
"Show kind attention to the reckless opponents
of Christianity on the bed of sickness and pain,
and they never can become your personal enemies.   Here, if any where, love begets love."
Guided by such sentiments in his intercourse
with the Bakwains, Livingstone acquired great

influence among them; yet he depended entirely upon persuasion. He taught them both publicly and in private conversation that he wished them to follow their own sense of right and wrong, and not to be governed by any desire to please him. Such was the respect paid to his opinion, that in five instances it was positively known that his influence prevented war.

All the natives of Africa are slow in coming to a decision upon religious subjects. In matters which have not come within the range of their observation they are somewhat stupid, but in their own worldly affairs they are very shrewd and intelligent. Their knowledge of cattle, sheep, and goats, of the pasture suited to each, and of the varieties of soil best suited to the different kinds of grain, is very accurate.

The English traders, who are sure to come wherever a missionary lives, sold guns and ammunition to the Bakwains; and this excited so much alarm among the neighboring Boers that when the number of guns amounted to five they planned an expedition of several hundred men to capture them. Knowing that the Bakwains would rather fly to the desert than give up their fire-arms and become slaves, Livingstone went to the commandant, Mr. Gert Krieger, and by representing the evils of such an expedition, per-

suaded him to defer it ; but in return he desired
the missionary to act as a spy over the Bakwains. He explained the impossibility of doing
so by referring to an instance which occurred
soon after he came to live with them, in which
Sechele had gone with his whole force to punish
an under chief, without his knowledge. A man
whose name was Kake rebelled against the chief,
and maltreated some natives who remained faith-
ful to him. Sechele consulted Livingstone, and
he advised mild measures ; but the messengers
sent to Kake were taunted with the words, " He
only pretends to wish to follow the advice of the
teacher. Sechele is a coward—let him come and
fight, if he dare."

The next time the offense was repeated Sechele told Livingstone he was going to hunt elephants, and asked the loan of a black metal pot
for cooking, as theirs of pottery are very brittle.
He gave it, and a handful of salt, with the request for two titbits—the proboscis and forefoot
of the elephant. Nothing more was heard, till
he saw the Bakwains carrying home the wounded,
and heard some of the women uttering the loud
wail of sorrow for the dead, while others pealed
forth the shout of victory. Then it came out
that Sechele had attacked and driven away the
rebel.

This story told the commandant, soon grew to very formidable proportions among the Boers. The five guns of the Bakwains became five hundred, and the black pot was magnified to a cannon, the loan of which the missionary had confessed ; and on this ground a letter was sent to the other missionaries in the South, demanding his immediate recall. The same story was told the Colonial Government, with grave assurance of its truth. These Boers, it would seem, though less enlightened, are not altogether unlike the people of our own country. Right around us there are people who have the faculty of magnifying a story much like that—the smallest matter in their hands rapidly gathers huge proportions, like the rolling snow-ball of the school-boys, which we often see; but it vanishes in the light of truth as that snow-ball melts away beneath a vernal sun.

The Boers often sent letters to Sechele, ordering him to come and surrender himself as their vassal, and put a stop to the English traders going into the country with fire-arms for sale. But he replied, "I was made an independent chief, and placed here by God, and not by you. I was never conquered by Mosilikatze, as those tribes whom you rule over, and the English are my friends. I get every thing I wish from them.

I can not hinder them from going where they like." A little further on we shall speak of the discovery of Lake Ngami—pronounced *Ingami,* with the first I as soft and short as possible. This discovery opened up a rich country for trade, and the traders came in fivefold greater numbers than ever.

The myth of the black pot had some good effect, for the Boers were for several years prevented from making any foray in the direction of Kolobeng, by the supposition that the Bakwains had artillery.

Every man in these tribes feels bound to tell his chief every thing which comes to his knowledge; and when questioned by a stranger he makes such answer as will please the chief, or such as shows the utmost stupidity. It was owing to this custom, probably, that the story arose representing the Bechuanas as so stupid they could not count ten; and this was about the very time when Sechele's father counted out one thousand head of cattle as a beginning of stock for his son.

As the Boers were constantly questioning his people about the guns and the cannon, Sechele asked Livingstone how they ought to answer. He replied, "Tell the truth." Then every one, whenever questioned, declared there was no can-

non among them; and the Boers, judging this
answer by what they would themselves have
said in the same circumstances, were confirmed
in the opinion that the Bakwains had artillery.

At last, however, they determined to disperse
the Bakwains, and drive out the missionaries, in
order to prevent the traders going past Kolobeng
to the country beyond. Their independence having been proclaimed by Sir George Cathcart, a
treaty was entered into with them, which provided that no slavery should be allowed in the
independent territory, and which secured the free
passage of Englishmen through the country.

"But what about the missionaries?" inquired
the Boers; when the "Commissioner" is said to
have replied—perhaps in a joke—"*You may do
as you please with them.*" This remark, circu-
lated by designing men, and generally believed
to express the real sentiment of the Colonial
authorities, doubtless led to the destruction of
three mission stations soon after.

During the long droughts at Kolobeng Livingstone was dependent on Kuruman for supplies
of corn; and at one time the family were re-
duced to living on bran. This they ground three
times over, to make fine meal from it. Animal
food was found there a greater necessary of life
than vegetarians would imagine. By right of

chieftainship Sechele had the breast of every
animal slaughtered by any member of the tribe,
at home or abroad, and he very kindly sent a
liberal share to the missionary family, during the
whole of their stay.   But these supplies were
irregular, so that they sometimes were glad to
accept a dish of locusts.   They have a strong
vegetable taste, the flavor varying with the
plants on which they chance to feed.   Roasted
and pounded into meal, with a little salt, they
are palatable.   Thus prepared, they keep for
months.   Our friend the missionary says of
them : " Boiled, they are disagreeable ; but when
they are roasted, I should much prefer locusts to
shrimps, though I would avoid both, if possible."

When suffering from want of meat, the children of our missionary ate, and seemed to relish,
a large kind of caterpillar which the natives gave
them.   These insects could not be unwholesome,
for the natives devoured them in large quantities.

These young Britons often turned Frenchmen,
and ate with eagerness a very large frog, called
" Matlametlo,"* which, when cooked, looks like a
chicken.   The natives suppose them to fall from

---

*The *Pyxicephalus adspersus* of Doctor Smith. Length of
head and body, five and a half inches; fore legs, three inches;
hind legs, six inches. Width of head posteriorly, three inches;
of body, four and a half inches.

the thunder-clouds, because immediately after a thunder-shower the pools which are filled and retain water a few days are alive with the noisy croakers. This occurs, too, in the dryest part of the desert, where an ordinary observer would find no sign of life. This enormous frog digs a hole at the root of certain bushes, and there ensconces himself during the months of drought. As he seldom comes out, a large spider takes advantage of the hole to weave his web across, and thus furnishes the owner of the dwelling with a screen and window gratis; and during the thunder-shower, which fills the hollows, while the Bechuanas are cowering under their skin garments, these matlametlo rush out from their hiding-places, and their sudden chorus, struck up at once on all sides, gives the impression of their descent from the clouds.

In trying to benefit the tribes living under the Boers of the Cashan Mountains, Livingstone twice made a journey of about three hundred miles to the east of Kolobeng. Sechele's independence and love of the English had made him very obnoxious to the Boers; and hence, he dare not trust himself among them, though anxious to accompany our missionary on these journeys. In the last journey, when they parted at the river Marikwe, Sechele expressed his regret that he

4

could not go himself, and gave Livingstone two
servants, with the remark, " These are to be my
arms, to serve you."   Said Livingstone, " Suppose we went North, would you come ?"   He
then told the story of Sebituane's saving his life,
and talked at length of the far-famed generosity
of that really great man. • It was then that the
thought of crossing the desert to Lake Ngami
first entered the mind of our missionary traveler.
Having formed his purpose, he began to collect all possible information about the desert.
Sekomi, the chief of the Bamangwato, had a
route, the knowledge of which he kept a secret,
because the lake country abounded in ivory, and
he obtained thence large quantities at small cost.
Sechele, always keenly alive to his own interest,
was anxious to get a share in that inviting field.
He had, too, a very strong desire to visit Sebituane, in part from a wish to exhibit his new at-
tainments in learning, but more from exalted
ideas of the benefits he would receive from the
liberality of that renowned chieftain.

At Livingstone's suggestion Sechele sent men
to Sekomi, asking permission to pass along his
path.   The request being accompanied with the
present of an ox to Sekomi, his mother, who has
great influence over him, refused, because she
had not been propitiated.   Then the most hon-

orable man in the tribe, next to Sechele, was sent with an ox for both Sekomi and his mother; and this was met with refusal. It was said, "The Matebele, the mortal enemies of the Bechuana, are in the direction of the lake, and should they kill the white man, we shall incur great blame from all his nation."

There are among these tribes vestiges of ancient partitions and lordships. When the original tribe broke up into Bakwains, Bamangwato, and Bangwaketse, the Bakwains retained the hereditary chieftainship. So their chief, Sechele, possesses certain advantages over Sekomi, the chief of the Bamangwato.. If they were hunting together, Sechele's right would give him the heads of all game killed by Sekomi.

Sechele's father received the chieftainship from an elder brother, who, becoming blind, gave it to him. The descendants of this man pay no tribute to Sechele; and though he is the actual ruler, and in every other respect supreme, yet Sechele calls him Kosi, or chief. The other tribes will not taste pumpkins of a new crop till the Bahurutse have "bitten it." They celebrate the occasion with a public ceremony, and the son of their chief first tastes of the new harvest.

The Kalahari Desert lay between the Bakwain country and Lake Ngami. Many attempts had been made by the natives to reach the lake through the desert, but without success. This desert is a large tract of very flat country, without running water, and it is very difficult to obtain enough of the precious liquid from wells to quench thirst. The desert is by no means destitute of vegetation or inhabitants. Vast herds ōf a certain species of antelope roam over these plains, and large quantities of grass grow upon them, with occasionally large patches of bushes, and even trees. The human inhabitants are Bushmen and Bakalahari. The soil is for the most part light-colored, soft sand—nearly pure silicia. The beds of the ancient rivers contain alluvial soil, which, baked by the sun, holds the rain-water in pools for several months of the year. A plant called leroshua grows here, which is a great blessing to the inhabitants of the desert. It is a small plant, with a stalk not thicker than a crow's quill, with linear leaves. On digging down a foot ōr eighteen inches a tuber is found, often large as the head of a young child, and when the rind is taken off it is found to be a mass of cellular tissue, filled with juice much like that of a young turnip; and because of its depth beneath the soil it is delightfully cool and refreshing.

There is a large number of these plants with tuberous roots, and there is an example of a plant not tuber-bearing in other circumstances becoming so here, where the tuber is necessary as a reservoir of moisture to preserve the life of the plant through the long droughts. The plant is one of the melon species, bearing a small, scarlet-colored, eatable fruit, like the cucumber. In other parts of the country, where long heat burns the soil, a plant called Mokuri is found, which deposits under ground a number of tubers, some of which are large as a man's head. They are found about a yard from the stem, in a circle around it. The natives strike the ground with stones on the circumference of the circle, till by the difference in the sound they know the water-bearing tuber to be beneath. They then dig a foot or so, and find it.

But the most remarkable plant of the desert is the *kengwe*, or *keme*—the water-melon. When more than the usual quantity of rain falls, vast tracts of country are literally covered with these melons. This was the case every year, when the amount of rain was greater than now. Then the Bakwains could cross the desert, and they sent trading parties to the lake every year. Now, this abundant crop of melons occurs usually once in ten or eleven years. Then man rejoices in the rich supply of food. The elephant, true lord of the forest, revels in the rich pasturage afforded

by the vast fields covered with this fruit; and
animals of every kind—the rhinoceros, antelope,
lion, hyena, jackal, and mice—all enjoy and appreciate the common blessing. These melons are
not all eatable. Some are sweet, and some bitter,
so that the whole are called by the Boers the
" bitter water-melon." The natives select them
by striking them with the hatchet, and applying
the tongue to the gashes. The sweet are quite
wholesome, while the bitter are unhealthy food.
Another like instance of one species of plants
bearing both sweet and bitter fruits, is found in
this country in the red cucumber. Melons in
the garden may be made bitter by a few bitter
kengwe in the vicinity. The bees convey the
pollen from one to the other.

Livingstone having communicated his intention of attempting a journey to Lake Ngami, to
Colonel Steele, aiddecamp to the Marquis of
Tweedale, at Madras, he made it known to two
other gentlemen, whose friendship had been
gained during their African travel, Major Vardon, and Mr. Oswell. All of these gentlemen
were very fond of African travel and discovery.
And the two former must have envied Mr. Oswell
his good fortune in being able to leave India, to
enter upon the hardships and pleasures of desert
life. He left his high position at very consider-

able pecuniary sacrifice, with no other desire than to extend the boundaries of geographical knowledge. Before Livingstone knew of his coming, he had arranged with Sechele to pay for the guides he furnished, by the loan of a wagon to bring back whatever ivory they might obtain from the chief at the lake. Mr. Oswell came, however, bringing Mr. Murray with him, and generously assumed the entire expenses of the guides. Sechele himself would gladly have accompanied them, but fearing the attack of the Boers, Livingstone dissuaded him from the purpose, lest he might incur blame for taking the chief away.

Just before the arrival of Oswell and Murray, who came the last of May, a party came to Kolobeng from the lake, sent by the chief Lechulatebe, to invite the missionary to visit that country. These people brought flaming accounts of the vast quantities of ivory to be found there; which inspired the Bakwain guides with great eagerness for the success of the expedition.

On the first of June, 1849, a fair start was made for the unknown region. Moving northward, through a range of tree-covered hills, to Shokuane, the former home of the Bakwains, they soon after entered the high road to the Bamangwato country. This road, for the most part, follows an ancient river-bed, and leads northward. The surrounding country is perfectly flat, but covered with open forest and bush, and abundance of grass. The trees are mostly "Monato"— a kind of acacia. A large caterpillar, called "Nato," feeds upon the leaves of these trees by night, and comes down in the day-time to bury itself in the sand at the root. When about to pass into the chrysalis state, it buries itself in the soil, and, if left undisturbed, comes forth a beautiful butterfly. This change in the form of insect life, with which all my readers are familiar, was used with good effect by our missionary, when speaking to the natives, to illustrate our own great change and resurrection.

Passing Lopepe on this journey, Livingstone noticed additional evidence to that before gathered of the desiccation of the country. The first time he passed here it was a large pool, with a stream flowing out of it to the south. Now it was difficult to obtain water for the cattle by digging in the bottom of a well. At Mashue a never-failing supply of pure water was found in a sandstone, rocky hollow. Here our travelers left the Bamangwato road, and struck off to the north into the desert. The country is covered with bushes and trees, of a kind of leguminosæ, with lilac flowers.

The soil is soft white sand, in which the wheels of the wagon sink over the felloes, making very hard work for the oxen. When they came to Serotli they found only a few hollows, like those made by the buffalo and rhinoceros, when they roll themselves in the mud. In the corner of one of these a little water appeared. The dogs would have quickly lapped it all up, if they had not been driven away. And this was, in appearance, the only supply for a score of men, twenty horses, and about eighty oxen. However, Ramotobi, the chief guide, who had spent his youth in the desert, declared there was plenty of water to be had. This place must afford the only supply of water they could expect for the next seventy miles— three days' journey. And the prospect was not flattering. The spades were brought out, but the guides, despising such aid, began scooping out the sand with their hands. By the aid of both hands and spades, the sand was at last dug out of two holes, so as to form pits about six feet deep, and as many in width. The guides were very earnest in their injunctions not to break through the hard stratum of sand. If this were broken, they said, "the water would go away."

An Englishman traveling in this country proved the value of such advice by disregarding it. He dug through the sandy stratum forming the

bottom of the wells, and thus destroyed them.
Our travelers found that the water flowed in from
all sides, at the line of contact between the soft
sand and this flooring of incipient sandstone.
Waiting for it to collect, they had enough that
evening for the horses.   But the thirsty oxen,
who had been without water four full days, had
to be taken back to Lobotani for a supply.   The
next morning it was found that the water had
flowed in faster than at first—affording a sufficient supply for all their need.

In the evening of their second day at Serotli,
a hyena raised a panic among the cattle, by ap-
pearing suddenly amidst the grass.   This cowardly animal always adopts such a mode of attack.
If an animal is running away he will bite ; but if
the animal stands still, so does he.   Seventeen
of their draught oxen ran away, and, in their
flight, went into the hands of Sekomi.   And as
this chief was unfriendly to their success in this
expedition, they did not very much desire to see
him.   But Sekomi sent back the oxen with a
message, strongly urging Livingstone to abandon
his scheme of crossing the desert.   "Where are
you going ?   You will be killed by the sun and
thirst, and then all the white men will blame me
for not saving you."   Our travelers replied that
the white men would attribute their death to their

own stupidity and "hard-headedness." They sent
a handsome present to Sekomi, with the promise
of a repetition on their return, if he allowed the
Bakalahari to keep the wells open for them.

After exhausting all his eloquence in fruitless
efforts to persuade the party to return, the under-
chief, who headed the band of messengers from
Sakomi, inquired, "Who is taking them?" Looking round, he exclaimed with an expression of
deep disgust, "It is Ramatobi!" This guide was
a fugitive from Sekomi's tribe, who had fled to
Sechele. But though engaged in what he knew
was opposed to the interests of his own tribe, he
was in no danger; since these desertions from
one tribe to another were quite common. The
fugitive may even visit the tribe from which he
escaped without harm.

Here in the desert, where no water was ac-
cessible, large numbers of elands, fat and sleek
as if fully supplied in all their wants, fed around
our travelers. And when they killed some of
these fine animals, their stomachs contained considerable quantities of water. These animals
subsist for months together without drinking—
having only the moisture of the pasturage on
which they feed. But when the drought is such
as completely to dry up the sap of vegetation, as
occasionally happens, they are driven from the

desert. The presence of these animals give the experienced traveler of the desert no assurance against the danger of perishing with thirst. But if he falls upon the "spoor," or track of the buffalo, rhinoceros, or zebra, he knows that, following it a few miles, water is certain to be found.

There is here such perfect sameness in the landscape, in whatever direction you look, that if you walk a quarter of a mile from the wells, it is difficult to return. The country is perfectly flat, and the soil a soft white sand. A peculiar glare of bright sunlight from a cloudless sky everywhere meets the eye. One clump of trees and bushes, with the open spaces between, looks so exactly like another, that those who have spent their lives in the desert, sometimes lose their way. While here at Serotli, Oswell and Murray went out one day to hunt an eland, taking one of the Bakalahari for a guide. Even this son of the desert was so puzzled with the perfect sameness of the country, that the party wandered about all night in the cold, vainly trying to find their way back to the wagons. The next day, however, the hunters succeeded in making a return by their own sagacity—which is greatly quickened by sojourn in the desert.

Livingstone sometimes felt much annoyed at the low estimation in which his hunting friends were held by the natives. "Have these hunters who come so far, and work so hard, no meat at home?" said they. "Why, these men are rich," was the reply, "and could slaughter oxen every day of their lives; and yet they come here and endure so much thirst for the sake of this dry meat, none of which is equal to beef!" "Yes, it is for the sake of play besides"—the idea of sport is not in their language. This produces a laugh, as much as to say, "Ah! you know better;" or, "Your friends are fools."

Our travelers left Serotli in the afternoon, and the second night found they had made only twenty-five miles. The distance was measured by a trocheameter, an instrument which, when fastened to the wagon wheel, records the number of its revolutions. This number, multiplied by the circumference of the wheel, gives the actual distance traveled over.

Ramotobi, the guide, was angry at this slow progress, and said, "If we travel so slowly we shall never reach the next water, which is three days in front." The wagons dragged very heavily through the deep sand, and even though it was Winter, the sun was so hot that the oxen could travel only morning and evening, so that next day, with the utmost efforts of the servants, screaming, cracking their whips, and beating the tired oxen, they were able to urge them only nineteen miles. As near as could be determined, they still had about thirty miles of the same dry work between them and the next water. At this season the grass becomes so dry that it crumbles to powder in the hands; so the oxen stood wearily chewing, without taking a single fresh mouthful, sometimes lowing painfully as they caught the smell of water from the vessels in the wagons.

But these brave men had no thought of being defeated in their purpose, and accordingly Murray and the guide started forward with the horses, so as to save them for a desperate effort, in case the oxen should fail, while Livingstone and Oswell remained to bring their wagons on their track as far as the oxen could drag them, and then send the cattle forward, too.

The horses walked quickly away, but on the next morning, when they supposed the steeds had nearly reached the water, they were discovered just along side of the wagons. Ramotobi, having come across the fresh footprints of some Bushmen, turned aside to follow them, though they led in an opposite direction to the course our travelers wished to go. Murray followed the guide trustingly, saw him slaughter an antelope which had been caught in one of the Bushmen's

WARRIOR AND WIFE.

pitfalls, and after a hard day's ride found himself close upon the wagons.

Though for sixty or seventy miles along their path one clump of bushes and trees seemed exactly like every other, still Ramotobi showed an admirable knowledge of the trackless waste of shrub. Walking along beside Livingstone this morning, he said, "When we come to that hollow we shall light upon the highway of Sekomi, and beyond that, again, lies the river Mokoko." Some of the men, going forward on a little path where were some of the water-loving animals, returned with the joyful news of "*watse*"—water— showing the mud upon their knees in confirmation of the tidings. This proved to be a pool of delicious rain-water, called Mathuluani. The supply of water it afforded was welcomed with thankfulness by the weary travelers. The thirsty oxen rushed into the pool till the water was deep enough to be nearly level with their throats, and then stood drawing in the long refreshing mouthfuls till their sides, just now collapsed, were distended as if they would burst. This was in the bed of the river Mokoko, though Livingstone could not perceive it to be a river-bed at all. The name refers to the water-bearing stratum before spoken of.

Resting here awhile, our travelers then passed

along the river-bed to Mokokonyani, where the water, generally under ground, makes its appearance on the surface. Three miles further down is another spring, called Lotlakani—a little seed. Here Livingstone met with the first Palmyra trees he had seen in South Africa. They were twenty-six in number.

When leaving the Mokoko Ramotobi for the first time seemed at a loss which direction to take. Mr. Oswell, riding in front of the wagons, chanced to spy a bush woman running in a bent position to escape observation. Thinking it to be a lion, he galloped up to her. She thought herself captured, and began to give up her property, consisting of a few traps made of cords. Livingstone soon explained to her that they only wanted water, and would pay her if she would lead them to it. She consented, and though it was then late in the afternoon, she walked briskly in front of their horses, and conducted them a distance of eight miles, to the spring of Nchokotsa. She had fled from a party of her countrymen, and was now living far from all others, with her husband. Having led them to the water, she wished to return, but as it was now dark, our travelers desired her to remain. As she believed herself a captive, they thought she might slip away by night. And in order that she might not go away with the impression that they were dishonest, the travelers gave her a piece of meat and a large bunch of beads. At the sight of the beads she burst into a merry laugh, and remained very contentedly.

And now a word or two about these Bushmen—the tribe to which this woman belonged. They were probably the aboriginals of the southern part of the continent. They live in the desert from choice, and have an intense love of liberty. They never cultivate the soil, but live on game, and the roots and fruits of the desert, gathered by the women. The Bakalahari also inhabit the desert. Living upon the same plains, subjected to similar influences of climate for centuries, eating the same food, and enduring the same thirst, with the Bushmen; still the distinction between the two races remains.

The Bakalahari are said to be the oldest of the Bechuana tribes, and once possessed enormous herds of horned cattle. They live in the desert to escape their enemies; but retain the Bechuana love for agriculture and domestic animals. They till their gardens, though often they can hope for nothing more than a supply of pumpkins and melons. They give great care to the raising of small herds of goats, though sometimes obliged to lift water for them from small wells, with a bit of ostrich egg-shell, or by spoonfuls. For the most part they attach themselves to men of influence, in the different Bechuana tribes, around their desert home. From these they obtain spears, knives, tobacco, and dogs, in exchange for skins of animals which they kill. They are a timid race. A few Bechuanas may go into one of their villages and domineer over the whole community as they please. But they are compelled to change their manner when they meet the bold and fearless Bushmen. Their request for tobacco is at once respected, because these free sons of the desert would not hesitate to enforce that request with a poisoned arrow.

To escape visits from strange tribes of the Bechuanas, the Bakalahari make their homes far from water. They frequently hide their supplies of water in pits, which they fill with sand, and then build a fire over the spot. The women draw the water, carrying it upon their backs in water-vessels, twenty or thirty of which are inclosed in a bag or net. The water-vessel is an ostrich egg-shell, with a hole in one end, about the size of your finger. The water is pumped into these in a way somewhat peculiar. A hollow reed, about two feet long, and the mouth of the woman constitutes the pump. A bunch of grass is fastened to one end of the reed, and this inserted in a hole dug as deep as the arm will reach. Then the wet sand is packed down firmly around it. The woman now applies her mouth to the top of the reed. A vacuum is produced in the grass. The water collects there, and soon rises to the mouth. From the mouth a straw guides it to an egg-shell conveniently placed. Thus mouthful after mouthful is patiently pumped up till all the shells are filled. Then the whole is carried home in the manner mentioned and carefully buried. Livingstone says: "I have come into villages where, had we acted a domineering part, and rummaged every hut, we should have found nothing. But by sitting down quietly, and waiting with patience till the villagers were led to form a favorable opinion of us, a woman would bring out a shell full of the precious fluid, from I know not where."

CHAPTER III.

A T Nehokotsa our travelers found the first of
a large number of saliners, or salt-pans.
They are covered with an efflorescence of lime—
probably the nitrate.   This one is twenty miles
in circumference.   On the approach from the
south-east it is hidden by a thick belt of mopane
trees. Livingstone thus describes the first view
of it by himself and his companions: "At the
time the pan burst upon our view the setting sun
was casting a beautiful blue haze over the white
incrustations, making the whole look exactly like
a lake.   Oswell threw his hat up in the air at the
sight, and shouted out a huzza which made the
poor Bushwoman and the Bakwains think him
mad.   I was a little behind him, and was as completely deceived as he ; but as we had agreed to
allow each other to behold the lake at the same
instant, I felt a little chagrined that he had unin-
tentionally got the first glance.   We had no idea

that the long-looked-for lake was still more than three hundred miles distant. One reason of our mistake was that the river Zonga was often spoken of by the same name as the lake; namely, Nokâ ea Batletli—River of the Batletli.

"The mirage on these salines is marvelous. It is never, I believe, seen in perfection, except over such saline incrustations. Here not a particle of imagination was necessary for realizing the exact picture of large collections of water— the waves danced along above, and the shadows of the trees were vividly reflected beneath the surface in such an admirable manner that the loose cattle, whose thirst had not been slaked sufficiently by the very brackish water of Nehokotsa, with the horses, dogs, and even the Hottentots, ran off toward the deceitful pools. A herd of zebras in the mirage looked so exactly like elephants that Oswell began to saddle a horse in order to hunt them; but a sort of break in the haze dispelled the illusion. Looking to the west and north-west from Nehokotsa, we could see columns of black smoke, exactly like those from a steam-engine, and were assured that they arose from the burning reeds of the Noka ea Batletli."

On the Fourth of July they went forward on horseback toward what they supposed to be the lake. Again and again did they seem to see it ;

but at last they came to the veritable water of
the Zouga, which they found to be a river running to the north-east. On the opposite bank
was a village of Bahurutse, a tribe who live among
the Batletli. They seem to be allied to the Hottentot family. Sebituane found them in possession of large herds of the great-horned cattle.
Livingstone and two Bakwains waded across the
river by the side of a fishing-weir. In trying to
cross Mr. Oswell got his horse mired in the
swampy bank. The people were found to be
friendly, and informed the strangers that this
water came out of the Ngami. The travelers
might, they said, "be a moon on the way," but
they now had the river Zouga at their feet, and
by following it they would reach the "broad
water." This·was joyful news, and put the whole
company in fine spirits.

The next day, when their success made them
feel very kindly toward every one, two of the
Bamangwato came and sat by their fire. They
had been sent by Sekomi to drive away all the
Bushmen and Bakalahari from the path of the
travelers, so they could not assist or guide them.
These men seemed to feel no enmity, but entered
into friendly conversation. "You have reached
the river now," said they. Yet they still continued to fulfill the instructions of their chief.

Going up the Zouga in advance of Livingstone and his company, they spread the report that his object was to plunder all the tribes living on the river and lake; but when about half-way up the river the principal man died of fever. The villagers connected his death with the attempt to injure Livingstone, and so it turned greatly to his advantage. They all understood, easily, the reasons Sekomi had for desiring the failure of the expedition.

When our travelers had ascended this beautiful river about ninety-six miles, and learned that they were still quite a distance from Ngami, they left all the wagons, except Mr. Oswell's, which was smallest, at Ngabisane. All the oxen but one team were left, that they might be recruited for the homeward journey.

Pushing onward toward the lake, they were kindly received by the Bakoba, whose language clearly shows their affinity to the tribes of the North. The chief of the lake sent orders to all the people on the river to assist the travelers. This tribe just named are a singular people. They are the Quakers of Africa; they have never been known to fight. They have a tradition that their forefathers, in their first attempts at war, made their bows of the Palma Christi, and when these broke they gave up fighting alto-

gether. They invariably submit to the rule of
every horde which overruns the river countries
where they dwell. They call themselves Bayeiye men, but the Bechuanas call them Bakoba—
a term which contains somewhat of the idea of
slaves.

A long time after Livingstone's visit, the chief
of the lake thought to make soldiers of them,
by furnishing them shields. "Ah! we never
had these before," said they; "that is the reason
we have always succumbed. Now we will fight."
But a marauding party came from the Makoloto,
and these "Friends" took to their canoes at once,
and paddled rapidly down the Zougo till they
reached the end of the river. The canoes of
these people are made from the trunks of trees
hollowed out with iron adzes. If the tree has a
bend so has the canoe. They have fires in these
rude crafts, and while on a journey, sleep in them.
"On land," say they, "you have lions, serpents,
hyenas, and your enemies; but in your canoe,
behind a bank of reed, nothing can harm you."
Livingstone's opinion of them is given in the following quotation, along with other matters per-
taining to our narrative: "I liked the frank and
manly bearing of these men, and instead of sitting in the wagon, preferred a seat in one of the
canoes. I found they regarded their rude vessels

as the Arab does his camel. . . . Their sub-
missive disposition leads to their villages being
frequently visited by hungry strangers. We had
a pot on the fire, in the canoe, by the way, and
when we drew near the village, devoured the contents. When fully satisfied ourselves, I found we
could all look upon any intruders with perfect
complacency, and show the pot in proof of having devoured the last morsel."

"While ascending in this way the beautifully
wooded river, we came to a large stream flowing
into it. This was the river Tamunak'le. I inquired whence it came. 'O, from a country full
of rivers—so many, no one can tell their number—and full of large trees.' This was the first
confirmation of statements I had heard from the
Bakwains, who had been with Sebituane, that the
country beyond was not the 'large sandy plateau'
of the philosophers. The prospect of a highway
capable of being traversed by boats to an entirely
unexplored and very populous region, grew, from
that time forward, stronger and stronger in my
mind ; so much so, that the actual discovery
seemed of but little importance. I find I wrote,
when the emotions caused by this magnificent
prospect of the new country were first awakened
in my breast, that they might subject me to the
charge of enthusiasm, a charge which I wished I

deserved, as nothing good or great had ever been accomplished in the world without it."

Twelve days had elapsed since the departure from Ngabisane, where the wagons were left— when our travelers reached the north-east end of Lake Ngami. On the first of August, 1849, Livingstone, Oswell, and Murray went down to the broad part. Then, for the first time, this beautiful sheet of water was seen by Europeans. The direction of the lake, by compass, seemed to be north north-east, and south south-west. The southern part is said to bend round to the west, and to receive the Teoughe from the north at the north-west extremity. No horizon could be seen off at the south south-west. The only means of estimating the extent of the lake was the statement of the natives that they traveled round it in three days. This would make the circumference about seventy-five miles. The water is too shallow to be of much importance as a highway of commerce. Livingstone asserts he "saw a native punting his canoe over seven or eight miles of the north-east end." For months preceding the annual supply of water from the north, the lake is so shallow that cattle approach the water through the low, boggy, reedy banks, with difficulty. Another of the numerous proofs of desiccation, so frequently met with throughout the country, was found here. On the west side of this arm of the lake there is a space devoid of trees, affording evidence that the water has receded thence at no very distant period. The Bayeiye asserted that when the annual inundation begins, not only trees of great size, but antelopes are swept down by the rushing waters. The trees are gradually driven to the opposite side by the wind, and are soon imbedded in the mud. The water of the lake is brackish when low, and perfectly fresh when full. The water of the Tamunak'le which flows into the Zouga was found to be clear, cold, and soft, as you ascend the river, so as to suggest the idea of melting snow.

Livingstone found this whole region much lower than that from which he came. The lowest point is Lake Kumadau, into which the waters of the Zouga flow, about two hundred miles from Lake Ngami. Here water boils at a point between 206° and 207½°, as indicated by Newman's Barometric thermometer. This gives an elevation of not much more than two thousand feet above the level of the sea. And that is two thousand feet below Kolobeng. This is the southern and lowest part of an extensive river system, which receives the floods from the north, produced by tropical rains; and which seems to have been prepared for a more abundant supply than now flows in these channels.

"It resembles a deserted Eastern garden, where all the embankments and canals for irrigation can be traced, but where the main dam and sluices having been allowed to get out of repair, only a small portion can be laid under water. In the case of the Zouga, the channel is perfect, but water enough to fill the whole channel never comes down, and before it finds its way much beyond Kumadau, the upper supply ceases to run, and the rest becomes evaporated. The higher parts of its bed even are much broader and more capacious toward Kumadau. The water is not absorbed so much as lost in filling up an empty channel, from which it is to be removed by the air and sun. There is, I am convinced, no such thing in the country as a river running into the sand, and becoming lost. The phenomenon, so convenient for geographers, haunted my fancy for years; but I have failed in discovering any thing except a most insignificant approach to it."

This phenomenon, which Livingstone, in the words now quoted, has *evaporated* into a myth, has been convenient for many others, besides the geographers; orators and essayists have repeatedly stated it as fact till illustrations and arguments based upon it pervade our literature. Henceforth it must probably be treated as fable.

The principal object had in view by our missionary in this journey to the lake was to visit Sebitnane, the great chief of the Makololo, who was said to live some two hundred miles beyond. They had now reached a half-tribe of the Bamangwato, called Batauana, whose chief was a young man named Lechulatebe. His father had been conquered by Sebituane, and he received part of his education while a captive among the Bayeiye. He was ransomed by his uncle, who, having collected a number of families together, abdicated the chieftainship in his favor. With something of the spirit of "Young America," this young African thought to show his ability, and signalize his coming into power by acting directly contrary to the judicious and sensible advice of his uncle.

When the travelers came, the uncle advised that they be treated handsomely. To do this according to the customs of the country required the present of an ox; and so this promising young chief presented them with a goat. Livingstone, better acquainted than his companions with the customs of the country, knew this to be an insult, and proposed to loose the animal and let him go. But the rest of the party objected, fearing to offend the chief by so bold a hint of his impoliteness.

They wished to purchase some oxen or goats for food, and Lechnlatebe offered them elephants' tusks. "No, we can not eat these," said they; "we want something to fill our stomachs." "Neither can I," he replied; "but I hear you white men are all very fond of these bones, so I offer them. I want to put the goats into my own stomach." The natives of this part of the country, having never before had a market for them, knew nothing of the value of these "bones," as they called the tusks; so they left them to rot with the other bones of the elephant, where he fell. A trader who accompanied Livingstone and his party was now purchasing ivory at the rate of ten large tusks for a musket worth thirteen shillings sterling; and in less than two years from this time not a man could be found who was not keenly alive to the great value of this commodity.

Immediately after his arrival at the lake, Livingstone had applied to Lechulatebe for guides to Sebitnane. But he was afraid of that chief, and wished to retain the superiority which the possession of fire-arms gave him; hence, he was anxious to prevent communication between the white men and that chieftain, lest they should sell him guns. Livingstone urged that he would inculcate peace—that Sebituane had been a father to this young chief and Sechele, and that he was anxious to see the white missionary; but all in vain. Lechulatebe offered him · all the ivory he needed. This being refused, he reluctantly promised to furnish the guides; but the next day, when the travelers were ready to start, they were met by an obstinate refusal, and men were sent to the Bayeiye with orders to refuse them a passage across the river.

Unwilling to be defeated, Livingstone tried hard to build a raft at the narrow part of the river; but the dry wood was so worm-eaten it would not bear the weight of a single person, and this project was abandoned after many hours of fruitless work in the water. Our missionary says: "I was not then aware of the number of alligators which exist in the Zouga, and never think of my labor in the water without feeling thankful that I escaped their jaws." With his usual generosity, Mr. Oswell now offered to go down and bring a boat from the Cape, for a future expedition, and the season being far advanced, the party determined to return South again for the present.

Coming down the river they had time to notice its banks, which are very beautiful, resem-

bling parts of the river Clyde above Glasgow.
They are sloping and grassy on one side, and
perpendicular on the other, to which the water
swings, and adorned along their margins with
magnificent trees.

The sloping banks are selected by the Bayeiye for pitfalls, which they make to entrap
animals as they come to drink. They are so
carefully covered that some of the party fell into
them while searching for them in order to prevent the cattle falling into them. If an ox sees
a hole he shuns it with the utmost care. Old
elephants sometimes go in advance of the herd,
and throw off the coverings from the pitfalls on
each side of the path down to the water; and
instances have been known in which, with remarkable sagacity, they have lifted their young
out of the trap.

Very large numbers of elephants were found
on the southern bank—somewhat smaller than
those farther south. They come to the river by
night, and while drinking throw large quantities
of water over themselves. While enjoying this
refreshment they may be heard screaming with
delight. They show their dread of pitfalls by
starting, on their return to the desert, in a
straight line, from which they never diverge till
eight or ten miles away.

Our travelers discovered here a beautiful wa
ter antelope—an entirely new species—of light
brownish-yellow color. It is unknown except in
the central, humid basin of Africa, and is never
found a mile from water. It is a noble-looking
animal, when, as is usual, it stands with head
erect, gazing at the approaching stranger. When
a retreat is decided upon it lowers its head, and
begins with a waddling trot, which is soon exchanged for a gallop, in which it springs lightly
over the bushes, or bounds through the water.

Livingstone returned to Kolobeng, and in
April, 1850, made a new start, in company with
Sechele—who had now a wagon of his own—
intending to cross the Zouga at its lower end,
and following up that river and the Tamunakle,
reach the country of Sebituane by that route.
Mrs. Livingstone and the three children accompanied him this time. Sechele separated from
them at the crossing of the river in order to
visit Lechulatebe. The missionary family, meanwhile, passed along the northern bank, cutting
their way through the forest with very great
labor. The Bayeiye kindly opened the pitfalls
whenever they knew of the approach of the
travelers. Still, as in many cases, their coming
was not known, and the pits were left concealed.
The loss of oxen by this means was very heavy.

On nearing the mouth of the Tamunak'le, information was received that the banks of that river abounded with the fly, called tsetse. The bite of this insect is very poisonous to cattle; and as its presence might have brought the wagons to a sudden halt, in the wilderness, where no food could be obtained for the family, the party were compelled to recross the Zouga, to escape the danger.

Here they learned, from the natives, that a party of Englishmen, who had come to the lake, in search of ivory, were all sick of fever. So turning back from their course, they traveled hurriedly down the river, about sixty miles, to render them assistance. On their arrival they learned with sorrow that one of the company had already died. This was Mr. Alfred Rider, an enterprising young artist, who had come, soon after its discovery, to make sketches of the lake and surrounding country. But fortunately, the rest recovered, by the aid of medicines and the skillful nursing of Mrs. Livingstone—the first English lady who ever visited the lake.

Sechele employed all his eloquence to induce Lechulatebe to furnish guides, for Livingstone to visit Sebituane on ox-back, while his family remained at Lake Ngami. At last he yielded; persuaded, however, not so much by argument, as by an intense desire for a superior London-made gun, possessed by the missionary. It was the gift of Lieutenant Arkwright, and valued very highly, both on that account, and because of the impossibility of replacing it. The young chief offered any number of elephants' tusks, and promised to furnish Mrs. Livingstone with meat, during the absence of her husband. So the gun was delivered to him, and the guides provided.

Preparations for the departure being complete, Dr. Livingstone took his wife out about six miles from town, in order to give her a view of the broad part of the lake. The next morning, when he expected to start on his journey, their little boy and girl were attacked with the fever. And on the day following, all their servants were taken with the same disease. The best remedy in such cases is a change of place. So they started at once for the pure air of the desert. Thus the visit to Sebituane was reluctantly deferred a second time. It was not abandoned, however. The gun was left as part payment for guides the next year.

Some mistake having occurred in the arrangement with Mr. Oswell, he reached the Zouga only in time to meet Livingstone's party on their return. He then employed the remainder of the season in hunting elephants. The natives pro-

nounced him the greatest adept at this art that
ever came to the country. He has been known
to kill four large male elephants a day. The
value of the tusks would be one hundred guineas.
This lordly animal is so worried by the presence
of a few barking dogs, that he is utterly incapable
of attending to man. He awkwardly attempts to
crush them by falling on his knees. Sometimes
he places his forehead against a tree, ten inches
in diameter, and by glancing first on one side,
and then on the other, he pushes it down before him, as though he thought in that way to
catch his enemies. Mr. Oswell hunted without
dogs. This gave the natives a high idea of English courage.

When Sebituane heard of these repeated attempts to visit him, he sent three detachments
of his men to Lechulatebe, Sechele, and Sekomi,
with a present of thirteen cows to each; requesting them to assist the white men to reach him.
But these chiefs pursued the usual African policy
in attempting to keep him out of view, and act
as his agents in purchasing the goods he wanted
with his ivory. Hence, Sechele permitted all the
messengers to leave Kolobeng during Livingstone's absence, on a visit to Kurruman.

When, however, he started on his third attempt
to reach the country of Sebituane, Sekomi was

unusually gracious, and furnished a guide. When the party reached Nchokotsa, they were in need of another guide, as no one of those they now had knew any thing of the path they wished to follow beyond that point. Fortunately, they found one of Sekomi's men here, who was well acquainted with the Bushmen in the country they were to pass through. Fortunately, too, he needed some assistance they were able to render. The main-spring of his gun was broken. And in return for his service as a guide, Livingstone undertook the repair of the gun. The other guides were liberally rewarded by Mr. Oswell.

The party now moved rapidly northward, over a hard, flat country, for several hundred miles. Several salt-pans were found; one of which is one hundred miles long, by fifteen wide. In each of these salt-pans there is a spring of brackish water, containing nitrate of soda.

At a place called Matlomagan-yana, or the "links," they found quite a chain of never-failing springs. Here were several families of Bushmen, quite unlike those of the Kalahari desert. Those are generally short, and of light-yellow color. These are tall, lusty, and of dark complexion. Blackness of the skin, it seems, is not produced by heat alone. But heat with moisture gives the darkest hue.

One of these Bushmen, named Shobo, was obtained as a guide over the desert between these
springs and the country of Sebituane. The
guide gave no hope of reaching water for a
month. But, providentially, some supplies were
sooner found in a chain of rain-water pools.
After leaving these, the prospect was the most
uninviting and dreary which one can possibly
imagine. No bird or insect enlivened the scene.
And the landscape was adorned with no vegetation, save a low shrub, in the deep sand.

To add to the gloom, on the second day
Shobo, the guide, wandered to all points of the
compass. He would follow the tracks of elephants, which had been here in the rainy season,
in every direction; then sitting down in the
path he would say, in his broken Sichuana language: "No water; all country only; Shobo
sleeps; he breaks down.; all country." Then
curling himself up, he would go to sleep. The
oxen were terribly tired and thirsty. On the
morning of the fourth day, after professing igno-
rance of every thing, Shobo disappeared.

The party went forward in the direction in
which they last saw him. About eleven o'clock
they began to see birds, and soon after found the
trail of a rhinoceros. At this the oxen were
unyoked, and apparently knowing the sign, they

rushed along to find water in the river Mahabe, which flows from the Tamunak'le, and lay off to the west. The water in the wagons had been wasted by one of the servants, and by afternoon very little remained for the children. Of the suffering and intense anxiety experienced at this time, the words of Livingstone will speak most appropriately: "This was a bitterly anxious night, and next morning the less there was of water, the more thirsty the little rogues became. The idea of their perishing before our eyes was terrible. It would almost have been a relief to me to have been reproached with being the entire cause of the catastrophe; but not one syllable of upbraiding was uttered by their mother, though the tearful eye told the agony within. In the afternoon of the fifth day, to our inexpressible relief, some of the men returned with a supply of that fluid, of which we had never before felt the true value."

When they came to the river Mahabe, Shobo made his appearance at the head of a party of Bayeiye. In order to show his importance before his new friends he walked boldly up, and commanded the whole cavalcade to stop, and bring forth fire and tobacco, then coolly sat down to smoke his pipe. The showing off was so inimitably natural that the whole party stopped

to admire the acting.   Shobo was a fine specimen
of that wonderful people, the Bushmen ; and notwithstanding his recent desertion of them, our
travelers all liked him.

On this journey forty-three fine oxen were lost
by the bite of the tsetse.   This insect is very
little larger than the common horse-fly.   It is
nearly of the dark-brown color of the honey-bee,
having three or four yellow bars across the back
part of the body.   Its bite is certain death to the
horse, dog, and ox.   Many large tribes on the
river Zambesi can keep no domestic animal
except the goat, because of this insect.   Yet its
bite is no more harmful to man or wild animals
than the bite of a musketo.   The children of
our missionary were bitten frequently, and suffered no harm.   Calves, while feeding upon the
milk of the cow, have a like impunity from
the poison ; and yet, strangely enough, if a dog
which has been bitten is fed on milk, that gives
no relief from the certain death which results
in all cases.   From this curious fact it was
thought possible that the poison might come
from some plant, instead of the insect ; but the
question was settled by Major Vardon, of the
Madras army, who rode a horse up to a hill
infested with tsetse, without allowing him to
graze ; and though he remained only long

NATIVE HOUSES.

enough to view the country around, and catch a few specimens of the insect on the horse, the noble animal died in ten days afterward. The *habitat* of this insect is very sharply defined. The south bank of the river Chobe is infested with them, while on the opposite bank, fifty yards distant, not one could be found.

The Makololo whom our travelers met on the Chobe were delighted to see them. Sebituane, the chief, was about twenty miles down the river. Livingstone and Oswell proceeded in canoes to his temporary residence. He had come quite a distance to Sesheke, soon as he heard the white men were in search of him; and now he had come one hundred miles farther, to welcome them to his country. He was on an island, with his principal men around him. When the travelers arrived the natives were engaged in singing. When the great chief was informed of the difficulties his visitors had encountered in reaching him, and their great joy at being now in his presence, he replied with an expression of his own delight at meeting them. He said: "Your cattle are all bitten with tsetse, and will certainly die; but never mind, I have oxen, and will give you as many as you need." He then presented them with an ox and a jar of honey, and put them in the care of Mahale, who had led the party of messengers to Kolobeng. Prepared skins of oxen, soft as cloth, were given them for covering at night; and as the dignity of the chief did not allow any thing to be returned to him, Mahale became the proprietor of these robes. He arrogated to himself, too, all the credit of this visit from the white men.

Sebituane was doubtless the greatest man in all that country. He was at this time about forty-five years of age, tall and wiry, slightly bald, and of an olive or coffee-and-milk color. He was one of the greatest warriors of Africa. Unlike other noted war chiefs, he always led his men to battle in person. When he approached the enemy, he felt the edge of his battle-ax and said, "Aha! it is sharp, and who ever turns his back on the enemy will feel its edge." And so fleet of foot was he that all his warriors knew there was no escape for the coward. In some cases of cowardice, he would allow the person to return home. Afterward calling him, he would say, "Ah, you prefer dying at home to dying in the field, do you? You shall have your desire." This was the signal for his immediate execution.

After various fortunes in war, he conquered all the black tribes over an immense territory, and made himself a dread to the terrible and ferocious Mosilikatse. But he never could trust that chief.

And as the Batoka, on the islands of the Zambesi, had ferried his enemies across the river, he made a rapid descent upon them, swept them all out of their island fastnesses, and placed sentinels along the river. Of the chiefs who escaped he said, " They love Mosilikatse ; let them live with him. The Zambesi is my line of defense." He had thus performed a good service to the country, by breaking down the old system, which prevented trade from penetrating the central valley.

This chief had the art of gaining the affections both of strangers and his own people. And by this means he kept himself informed of every thing which took place in the country. If a company of poor men came to his town to sell hoes, or skins, he soon formed their acquaintance. However unpromising in their appearance, he would surprise them by coming alone to them, when they were sitting far apart from the Makololo gentlemen, who surrounded the chief. Sitting down with them, he would inquire if they were hungry. Then ordering an attendant to bring meal, milk, and honey, he would mix them in their sight, to remove all suspicion from their minds, and make them feast on a lordly dish—perhaps for the first time in their lives. Their hearts thus won by his hospitality and affability, they were ready to give him all the information in their power. He never allowed a party of strangers to leave him without a present to each one, servants and all. Hence his praises resounded through the country. " He has a heart! he is wise," were the expressions usually heard respecting him.

But all this applause could not stay the approach of death. Soon after realizing his ardent desire to receive a visit from the white men, the great chief was taken with violent inflammation of the lungs, originating in an old wound received upon the battle-field. Livingstone saw his danger, but feared to administer medicine, lest in the event of death he should be blamed. He mentioned it to one of the Makololo doctors, who replied, " Your fear is prudent and wise ; this people would blame you." In the afternoon of the Sunday on which he died, after the usual religious service, our missionary, with his little boy Robert, visited the dying chief. " Come near," said he, "and see if I am any longer a man. I am done." Finding him thus sensible of his danger, the missionary assented, and added a single sentence respecting hope after death. " Why do you speak of death ?" said one of the newly arrived doctors, " Sebituane will never die." Had Livingstone persisted in his opinion, he would have made the impression that he wished for the death of the chief. After sitting with him some time, and

commending him to the mercy of God, he rose to
depart, when the dying man raised himself up a
little, and calling a servant, said, "Take Robert
to Maunku," one of his wives, "and tell her to
give him some milk." These were the last words
of the dying chieftain.* His last battle had been
fought, and his war-club laid aside forever.

Doctor Livingstone says of him: "He was
decidedly the best specimen of a native chief I
ever met. I never felt so much grieved by the
loss of a black man before ; and it was impossible not to follow him in thought into the world
of which he had just heard before he was called
away, and to realize somewhat of the feelings of
those who pray for the dead. The deep, dark
question of what is to become of such as he
must, however, be left where we find it, believing
that, assuredly, the "Judge of all the earth will
do right." He was buried according to the custom of the country—in his cattle pen—and the
·whole herd driven over and around the grave for
an hour or two, so as to obliterate it. Our travelers, before proceeding further, were obliged to
wait for the message from Ma-mochisane, the
daughter of the late chief, on whom, by her
father's will, the chieftainship now devolved. She
was living twelve days' journey farther north, but
when her message came it gave them perfect lib-

erty to visit any part of the country. They then proceeded to Sesheke, one hundred and thirty miles to the north-east ; and in the latter part of June, 1851, they were rewarded by the discovery of the Zambesi, in the center of the continent, where the existence of that river was previously unknown. Though this was in the dry season, the river was from three hundred to six hundred yards wide, and a deep, flowing stream. At the time of its annual inundation it rises to a perpendicular hight of twenty feet, and floods the country for fifteen or twenty miles in width. Mr. Oswell said he had never seen so fine a river, even in India.

No suitable locality for a missionary settlement among the Makololo could be found, because the healthy districts were entirely defenseless, and the safe places were so constantly and fearfully scourged with fever that it was too perilous to risk the residence of the missionary family there. There was now no hope that the Boers would permit the peaceable continuance of the mission among the Bakwains at Kolobeng. Hence Livingstone resolved to relieve his family from further exposure by sending them to England, while he should continue his explorations in search of a healthy district which might be made a center of civilization. Having been absent from the scenes of civilization for eleven years, he returned to Cape Town in April, 1852, and his family embarked for England. He promised on their departure to rejoin them in two years, but subsequently the demands of his work constrained him to a longer stay, and the separation was continued five years.

CHAPTER IV.

A Long Journey Begun—Attack of the Bakwains by
the Boers—Plundering of the Missionary's House—
Sechele—Hot Wind of the Desert—The Ostrich—
Mowana Trees—The Lion—Encounter Between
Three Lions and a Buffalo.

EARLY in June, 1852, the longest journey of the great African missionary began. This journey, endured for the cause of humanity and Christian civilization, extended from Cape Town, at the southern extremity of the continent, to St. Paul de Loando, on the western coast; and thence obliquely across South Central Africa to Kilimane, near the mouth of the Zambesi, on the eastern coast. In all this weary travel of more than four thousand miles the best conveyance was a heavy lumber wagon, drawn by ten oxen. Where a wagon could not be used, he rode an ox. This kind of African traveling is described as "a prolonged system of picnicing, excellent for the health, and agreeable to those who are not over-fastidious about trifles, and who delight in being in the open air." The route of our traveler lay northward, along the cone-shaped tract of land which constitutes the promontory of the Cape. He was attended on this journey by two Christian Bechuanas, from Kuruman—who were most excellent servants—by two Bakwain men, and two young girls, who, having come to the Cape as nurses for the children of our missionary, were now returning to their home at Kolobeng. Slowly they wound their way through the colony to Orange River. On crossing this river they entered the territory of the Griquas—a mixed race sprung from natives and Europeans. They were governed for many years by Waterboer, an elected chief. Immediately upon his election to the chieftainship he declared that no marauding should be permitted. The government of these tribes is not despotic; hence, in spite of this declaration, some of his principal men plundered some villages of Corannas, south of Orange River, whereupon the chief seized six of the ringleaders, summoned his counsel, tried, condemned, and publicly executed them. This vigorous vindication of law and justice was so obnoxious to some of his people that they raised an insurrection and attempted to depose him. The insurgents twice attacked Griqua Town, his capital, but his bravery defeated them; and during his long reign of thirty

years no marauding expedition ever afterward
left his territory. When firmly established in
power he entered into treaty with the Colonial
Government, and adhered to all its stipulations
with unswerving fidelity to the end of his reign.

Many hundreds of these Griquas, and of the
Bechuanas, who inhabit this same territory, have
become Christians through the teaching of missionaries, and are partially civilized. Our traveler was at first somewhat disappointed in them.
He did not find among them that high degree
of Christian simplicity and purity he had expected; but when he passed on to the heathen,
in those countries entirely beyond the reach of
missionary influence, and compared them with
these Christian natives, he "came to the conclusion that if the question were examined in the
most rigidly severe or scientific way, the change
effected by the missionary movement would be
considered unquestionably great."

•Before the missionaries came among them,
these Griquas and Bechuanas were clothed like
the Caffres. A lady's clothing consisted of a
bunch of leather strings, about eighteen inches
in length, hung from the waist in front, with a
prepared skin of a sheep or antelope covering the
shoulders. The garments of the men were even
more scanty; consisting of the same kind of man-

tle, and a piece of the same material about as large as the crown of a hat, worn in front. Now, these people attend church in decent garments, though somewhat poor and coarse, and behave with decorum. Sunday is well observed among them. And even in localities where no missionary lives, religious meetings are held with regularity. Children and adults are taught by the better educated. And no one is permitted to make profession of faith till he can read and understand the nature of the Christian religion. Our missionary tells us he does not wish any one to understand that these people are model Christians. He does not even claim that character for himself and others, who have grown up, as these people have not, in an atmosphere of Christian influence. He tells us "they are more stingy and greedy than the poor at home; but in many respects the two are exactly alike." He gives the testimony of an intelligent chief, which he thinks very nearly correct. On being asked what he thought of them, the chief replied, "You white men have no idea of how wicked we are; we know each other better than you; some feign belief to ingratiate themselves with the missionaries; some profess Christianity because they like the new system, which gives so much more importance to the poor, and desire that the old system may pass away, and the rest—a pretty large number — profess because they are really true believers."

When our traveler reached the mission station Kuruman, he found Mr. Moffat very busy in carrying through the press a copy of the Bible in the language of the Bechuanas. This devoted man had now been engaged as a missionary in Southern Africa for nearly forty years. For thirty years he had given attention to the study of this language, having in view the translation of the Word of God into the native tongue of these people, to whose religious instruction he consecrated his life. So copious is this language, that we are told that even this man, who has studied it so long, never spends a week at his work without discovering new words. The capability of the language is shown by the fact that the Pentateuch is expressed in Mr. Moffat's translation, with a considerably less number of words than are used in our English version ; and even in fewer words than in the Greek Septuagint. Yet this language is simple in its structure. And our traveler does not think its copiousness any proof that these people have declined from a former and higher state of civilization and culture.

Livingstone was detained at Kuruman about two weeks by the breaking of a wagon wheel.

Thus he was providentially prevented from being present at the attack of the Boers on the Bakwains, at Kolobeng. During his stay at Kuruman, news of this attack was brought by the wife of Sechele. That chief gave an account of the battle in a letter, sent by his wife to Mr. Moffat.

The Boers, numbering four hundred, were sent out by Mr. Pretorious, who had lately joined them. The natives, under Sechele, defended themselves bravely till the approach of night permitted them to flee to the mountains. During the battle Masebele, the wife of Sechele, who brought the news to Kuruman, was hidden with her infant in the cleft of a rock, over which a number of the Boers were firing. The muzzles of their guns were seen over her head at every discharge. Her child beginning to cry, she was terrified lest her hiding-place should be discovered, and took off her bracelets as playthings to quiet it. Sixty of the Bakwains were killed. A number of women, and about two hundred of the mission school children, were carried off into slavery.

In their defense the Bakwains killed a number of the enemy. And as this was the first time that Boers had been slain by Bechuanas, Livingstone received the credit of having taught them how to kill Boers. Hence, in revenge, his house was plundered ; which had stood in perfect safety

for years, under the protection of the natives.
The books of a good library—some of which had
been the companions of his boyhood, his solace
in solitude—were all spoiled by tearing out handfuls of leaves, and scattering them over the place.
His stock of medicines was smashed; and the
furniture and clothing of the family carried off and
sold at auction to pay the expense of the expedition.

Expressing his sorrow for the loss of his library, our missionary adds, with genuine English
pluck: "Yet, after all, the plundering only set
me entirely free for my expedition to the North,
and I have never since had a moment's concern
for any thing I left behind. The Boers resolved
to shut up the interior, and I determined to open
the country, and we shall see who have been
most successful in resolution, they or I."

The only excuse for this unjust and cruel attack upon Sechele was his independence, and his
refusal to prevent English traders from passing
through his territory.

The threats of vengeance against Livingstone,
made by the Boers, for his teaching the Bakwains to shed their blood, had such influence
upon the natives that no one could be found
willing to attend him in his journey, for fear of
being pursued by the Boers. After waiting for

months he at last found three wagon drivers willing to risk a journey to the North. These servants were the worst possible specimens of natives, who copy the vices without imitating the
virtues of civilized people; but there was no
choice, as these were the only men to be had,
and our traveler had waited so long he was glad
to get away on any terms. George Fleming, a
colored man, who was going, with the assistance
of a Cape Town merchant, to establish a trade
with the Makololo, had succeeded in procuring
an equal number of servants, and he joined our
missionary in the journey.

When they had proceeded about forty miles,
to Motito, they met Sechele, who told them he
was on his way to the "Queen of England," to
seek redress for the wrongs he had suffered from
the Boers, through the unjust policy of the Colonial Government. He used all his eloquence to
persuade Livingstone to accompany him. When
the difficulties of the journey were pointed out
to him, to urge him to abandon his project, he
asked, very pointedly: "Will not the Queen listen to me, supposing I should reach her?" Livingstone replied: "I believe she would listen, but
the difficulty is to reach her." "Well, I shall
reach her," said he, and with unshaken purpose
he ⋅proceeded on his way. When he reached

Bloemfontein he found the British army just returning from a battle with the Basutos, in which both parties claimed the victory. The army officers invited Sechele to dine with them, heard his story, and gave him a handsome sum of money to help him on his journey to England. When he reached the Cape, however, his resources were exhausted, and he was obliged to return to his own country, one thousand miles distant. Livingstone says of him: "He is very dark, and his people swear by 'Black Sechele.' He has great intelligence, reads well, and is a fluent speaker. Great numbers of the tribes formerly living under the Boers have taken refuge under his sway, and he is now greater in power than he was before the attack on Kolobeng."

Having bid adieu to Sechele, our travelers skirted along the Kalahara Desert, sometimes entering it, but taking care to give the Boers a wide berth. An unusual amount of rain having fallen this year there was a bountiful crop of melons. Mr. J. Macabe, whom Livingstone met on this journey, informed him that his cattle, in crossing the desert, had subsisted on this fruit for twenty-one days, without water.

During the dry seasons a hot wind blows over the desert from the north, which feels as though it came from an oven. It seldom continues more than three days at a time. When the missionaries first came to this country, a little over forty years since, this wind came loaded with a fine reddish sand. Now the sand does not accompany it, but it is so destitute of moisture that it causes the best English furniture and boxes to shrink, so that every wooden article imported to the country is warped. The electrical condition of this wind is such that a bunch of ostrich feathers held against it, for a few seconds only, becomes as strongly charged as if connected with a powerful electrical machine. When this hot wind is blowing, and occasionally at other times, the electrical condition of the atmosphere is such that the motion of a native in his kaross, or fur mantle, produces a stream of small brilliant sparks. Livingstone tells us the first time he noticed this phenomenon was when a chief was riding with him. Seeing a part of his mantle, which was exposed to friction by the motion of the wagon, assume a luminous appearance, Livingstone rubbed it briskly with his hand, when it gave out bright sparks, attended with a crackling sound. "Don't you see this?" said he. The chief replied: "The white men did not show us this. We had it long before white men came into the country—we and our forefathers of old."

They had witnessed this fact for ages, but it excited no inquiry among a people where the human mind has lain dormant and slumbering for centuries, and where hardly any subject is discussed, as Livingstone remarks, "except those which have an intimate connection with the wants of the stomach."

On the 31st of December, 1852, our travelers reached Litubaruba, Sechele's town. Near the village is a cave called Lepelole. It affords evidence of the existence, in former times, of a gushing fountain. This cave was thought by the natives to be the habitation of the Deity; and for this reason no one dared to enter it. When Livingstone proposed to explore the lohaheng, or cave, the old men said that every one who went in there remained forever, adding, "If the teacher is so mad as to kill himself, let him do so alone, we shall not be to blame." Sechele's declaration that he would follow wherever the teacher led filled the people with the greatest consternation. Thinking that those who were reported to have perished in the cave had fallen over some precipice, our traveler provided himself and company with lights, ladder, and lines, so as to be prepared for any such emergency. But it turned out to be only an open cave, with an entrance about ten feet square, contracting into two water-worn branches, and these terminating in round orifices, through which subterranean streams had flowed. This whole country adjacent to the desert, and reaching from Kuruman up to the latitude of Lake Ngami, has a climate of remarkable salubrity. Mr. Oswell thought it much superior to the climate of Peru. And our missionary says, "Were it not for the expense of the trip, I should have no hesitation in recommending the borders of the Kalahari Desert as admirably suited for all patients having pulmonary complaints. It is the complete antipodes to our cold, damp English climate."

Leaving the Bakwains, our travelers passed on in their northward journey to Motlatsa. Finding only a small supply of water here, they were obliged to send the oxen across the country to the deep well Nkauane. Half of the cattle were lost on the way to the well; and when found again they had been five days without water. On these plains, over which our missionary traveled, the ostrich is often seen quietly feeding on some spot where no one can approach him without being seen by his watchful eye. This bird seems to have a strange fancy that its only safety is to prevent its retreat from being cut off at the windward. So if it is feeding in a valley open at both ends, and a number of men commence running toward the end through which the wind comes, though the whole country is open for miles at the other end, yet he rushes on madly to get past the men, and thus is often speared. If he sees a wagon moving along a mile to the windward, he thinks it is a plan to entrap him, so he runs wildly to get past the train ; often coming so near the front oxen, that the travelers get a shot at the silly bird.   When his course is once chosen, he never turns from it, but only increases his speed.

When feeding, his pace is from twenty to twenty-two inches ; when walking, but not feeding, twenty-six inches ; when running in fright, it is from eleven and a half to fourteen feet.   Usually one can no more follow the motion of its legs with the eye than he can the spokes of a carriage wheel in rapid motion.   Livingstone estimates its speed at the rate of twenty-six miles an hour—equal to that of the express train on many of our railroads.

The ostrich begins to lay her eggs before finding a nest.   Hence, solitary eggs are found, lying forsaken all over the country, and becoming the prey of the jackals.   The nest, when one is selected, is only a hollow a few inches deep, and about three feet in diameter.   When the Bushmen find a nest, they carefully avoid touching the eggs, or leaving footprints near them.   They go up against the wind to the spot, carefully remove a few of the eggs, and by preventing suspicion, keep the ostrich laying for months, as domestic fowls are sometimes treated with us. The egg has very great vitality. One kept in a room at a temperature of 60° for three months was found to have a live chick in it partially developed. The flesh is white and coarse. When cooked, it resembles a tough turkey. When pursued by dogs, the ostrich has been known to turn upon them and inflict a kick forcible enough to break the dog's back.

The Bakalahari of Motlatsa were very friendly to our missionary, and listened with attention when he attempted to teach them in their own language. But at first, whenever he kneeled down to pray, and address an unseen being, the act and the position appeared so ludicrous to them, they could not refrain from laughter.

The most degraded of these tribes admit at once and universally the existence of God, and the doctrine of a future state. When intelligent men among the Bakwains were questioned respecting their knowledge of these subjects, they scouted the idea of ever having been without a pretty clear conception of God, and a future state of being, good and evil. They say they always regarded as sin all those things which the missionaries taught them to think sinful, except the having

more wives than one. Their having no form
of public worship, and showing so little reverence
for Deity, have doubtless led some to think them
entirely ignorant on these subjects.

Livingstone met an old Bushman at Lotlakani,
who he at first thought had no conception of
morality. After eating meat presented him by
the missionary, he sat by the fire relating his
adventures. Among these exploits was the killing five other Bushmen. "Two," said he, counting on his fingers, "were females, one a male, and
the other two calves." "What a villain you are,"
said the missionary, "to boast of killing women
and children of your own nation! What will God
say when you appear before him?" Much to
Livingstone's astonishment, he replied: "He will
say that I was a very clever fellow." But by further conversation the missionary found that
though he had been employing the word used
among the Bakwains for God, it was not the
word so used by the Bushman, who only meant
by it his Chief Sekomi. Had Livingstone known
the name of God in the Bushman tongue, the
mistake would probably never have occurred.

Leaving Motlatsa, our travelers passed down
the Mokoko, which was once a flowing stream.
Crossing the immense salt-pan Ntwetwe, they
unyoked the tired oxen about two miles beyond

its northern bank, under a fine specimen of the
Mowana-tree. It consisted of three branches
growing from one trunk. At the hight of three
feet from the ground it was eighty-five feet in circumference. Some French savans have argued
from the supposed age of these trees that they
must have been growing before the Flood; and
hence they reached the conclusion that "there was
no flood at all." But a careful examination made
by Livingstone shows, that upon the most liberal
estimate, made by counting the rings of the largest of these Mowana-trees, it can not be more
than one thousand, four hundred years old.
These trees have a wonderful vitality. The
natives make a strong cord from the fibers remaining in the bark when pounded; hence they
often strip the entire covering of bark from the
tree, as high as they can reach—but this does
not, by any means, kill the tree, as it would
almost any other. In a short time a new bark
is formed in the way of granulation, and the mischief repaired. This process of stripping off the
bark is so often repeated that it is not uncom-
mon to find the trunk, for five or six feet from
the ground, smaller in diameter by an inch or
two than it is farther up. Livingstone affirms
that no external injury—not even a fire—can
destroy this tree. He tells us he has seen

instances where it has grown in length after being
cut down and lying on the ground.   Neither can
the tree be destroyed by injury from within,
since they are often hollow, and have been found
with capacity to permit twenty or thirty men to
lie down and sleep within the hollow of the
trunk.

Trees called exogenous grow by successive
layers of woody fiber on the outside; in this
class the inside may be destroyed without affect-
ing the life of the tree.   Another class, called
endogenous, grows by layers on the inside, and
an injury to the outside has no effect upon the
vitality of the tree.   The mowana combines the
powers of both these classes.   Each of the lam-
inæ in this tree has its own independent vitality.
" In fact," says Livingstone, "the mowana is
rather a gigantic bulb run up to seed than a
tree."   The roots often extend along the surface
of the ground for forty yards from the trunk of
the tree, and retain their vitality after it is cut
down.   The wood is so soft and spongy that it
is difficult to draw out an ax struck in by a
strong arm.   Referring to the argument of the
French savan just mentioned, Livingstone says:
" I would back a true mowana-tree against a
dozen floods, provided you do not boil it in sea-
water; but I can not believe that any of these

now alive had a chance of being subjected to the experiment of even the Noachian deluge. Though it possesses amazing vitality, it is difficult to believe that this great baby-looking bulb, or tree, is as old as the pyramids."

The mopane-tree, which grows upon these plains, is remarkable for the little shade it affords. Its leaves fold together, and stand nearly perpendicular during the heat of the day, so that only their edges cast a shadow upon the ground. The larvæ of a small winged insect abound on these leaves, covered with a sweet gummy substance. The people use it for food, as they do also a large caterpillar, three inches long, which feeds upon these leaves. The natives have observed that this tree is more often struck by lightning than others. They say, "Lightning hates it," and caution travelers against seeking shelter under it when a thunder-storm is near. The wood is hard, and of a fine red color. It is called iron-wood by the Portuguese.

The morala-tree has three spines opposite each other on the branches. It has never been known to be struck with lightning, and is esteemed a sure protection against it. Such are the compensations of Providence. Protection is placed in immediate proximity with danger.

Slow progress was made in the journey for

some time, on account of the sickness of four of
the men of the party. At a place where the
travelers halted on this account, about the 19th
of March, the tall grass made the oxen very un-
easy, and one night they were frightened by a
hyena, and ran away into the forest. Livingstone's Bakwain lad ran away with them. He
had gone after the oxen to bring them back, but
lost them in the rush through the flat, trackless
forest. He followed their trail all the next day
and night, and on Sunday morning, when Livingstone was starting out in search of him he met
him. Kibopechoe, the lad, had found the cattle
on Saturday afternoon, had stood by them all
night, and had made his way through the forest
without compass or guide, driving about forty
oxen before him.

Soon after this the party reached the hill Ngua,
in south latitude 18° 27′, and longitude 24° 13′
east. This hill is three or four hundred feet
high, and being the first they had seen for many
weeks, our travelers felt like taking off their hats
to it. The valley on its northern side is pictur-
esque. The open glade is surrounded by forest
trees of various hues, while a little stream mean-
ders through the center. A herd of pallahs, or
antelopes, of reddish color, were standing on one
side, gazing at the strangers as they approached.

Zebras, gnus, and tressebes, in considerable numbers, were near by—some feeding carelessly, and
some putting on that air of displeasure which
these animals assume just before they resolve on
flight. A large white rhinoceros came along the
valley with his sauntering gait, without seeming
to notice the intruders. Several buffaloes stood
under the trees on the side of the valley opposite
the pallahs. Several of the party were sick, and
some not likely to recover. Our missionary says :
"It being Sunday, all was peace, and from the
circumstances in which our party was placed, we
could not but reflect on that second stage of our
existence, which we hope will lead us into scenes
of perfect beauty. If pardoned in that free way
the Bible promises, death will be a glorious thing ;
but to be consigned to wait for the Judgment-day
with nothing else to ponder on but sins we would
rather forget, is a cheerless prospect."

Livingstone's Bushmen now wanted to leave
him, and as there is little use in trying to thwart
such independent gentlemen as they, he paid them
and let them go. The payment, however, fasci-
nated some strangers who were present ; and they
volunteered to aid him. The game in this locality was very tame. Giraffes and koodoos gazed
with astonishment at our missionary whenever he
went out with the Bushmen. One morning at

day-break, a lion came and walked around the oxen again and again. Livingstone could only get an occasional glimpse at him from the wagon-box; but could not get a shot at him, though he was scarcely thirty yards distant. He roared at the top of his voice, to frighten the oxen. But they continuing to stand still, he at last became disgusted, and went away, his roar being still heard for some time in the distance. Our traveler could not see that he had any mane. And hence he thinks the maneless variety of this animal can use his voice as well as the others. Others were heard to roar, and when they could not raise a panic among the cattle, became angry, as could be observed in their tones.

Livingstone does not confirm with his testimony the prevalent notions of the "king of beasts." He says nothing he has learned of the lion would warrant the attributing to him either the nobleness or ferocity usually ascribed to him. A Newfoundland or St. Bernard dog he thinks has more nobility. The immense masses of muscle around the shoulders and jaws of the lion, proclaim his great strength. Still, in this respect, he would seem to be inferior to the tiger of India. The lion will sometimes take away an ox; but he does not carry it. He drags it on the ground. But here are the great traveler's own words: "To talk of the majestic roar of the lion is mere majestic twaddle. It is indeed well calculated to inspire fear, if you hear it in combination with the tremendously loud thunder of that country, on a night so pitchy dark that every flash of the intensely vivid lightning leaves you with the impression of stone blindness, while the rain pours down so fast that your fire goes out, leaving you without the protection of even a tree, or the chance of your gun going off. But when you are in a comfortable house or wagon, the case is very different, and you hear the roar of the lion without any awe or alarm. The silly ostrich makes a noise as loud, yet he was never feared by man. On my mentioning this fact some years ago, the assertion was doubted, so I have been careful ever since to inquire the opinions of Europeans, who have heard both, if they could detect any difference between the roar of a lion and that of an ostrich. The invariable answer was they could not, when the animal was at any distance. In general, the lion's voice seems to come deeper from the chest than that of the ostrich, but to this day I can distinguish between them with certainty, only by knowing that the ostrich roars by day, and the lion by night."

The African lion is of a tawny color, the male being adorned with a heavy mane, suggestive of great strength. · The face is not much like the usual drawings ; but the nose is prolonged like that of a dog. They are often seen in the daytime. When thus encountered by the traveler, the lion gazes a few seconds, turns around, and walks slowly away, looking back over his shoulder. Soon he begins to trot, and when he thinks himself out of sight, bounds off like a grayhound. When unmolested, there is very little danger of their attacking a man by day, or even in clear moonlight. When attacking an animal, the lion seizes him by the flank, near the hind leg, or by the throat. An eland may sometimes be seen so artistically and completely disemboweled by a lion that he seems hardly torn at all. The contents of the abdomen and chest thus taken out, make a full meal for the largest lion. The jackal, which comes sniffing around, sometimes receives a stroke from the lion's paw which lays him dead. When the lion is gorged with food, he falls into a sound sleep, and is then easily dispatched.

The reader will find interest in the account of an encounter between three lions and a wounded buffalo, narrated by an eye-witness :

"My South African journal is now before me, and I have got hold of the account of the lion and buffalo affair; here it is : 15th September, 1846. Oswell and I were riding this afternoon

along the banks of the Limpopo, when a water-
buck started in front of us. I dismounted, and
was following it through the jungle, when three
buffaloes got up, and after going a little distance,
stood still, and the nearest bull turned round. A
ball from the two-ouncer crashed into his shoulder, and they all three made off. Oswell and I
followed as soon as I had reloaded, and when we
were in sight of the buffalo, and gaining on him
at every stride, three lions leaped on the unfortunate brute ; he bellowed most lustily, as he kept
up a kind of running fight, but he was of course
soon overpowered and pulled down. We had a
fine view of the struggle, and saw the lions on
their hind legs tearing away with teeth and claws
in most ferocious style. We crept up within
thirty yards, and, kneeling down, blazed away at
the lions. My rifle was a single barrel, and I had
no spare gun. One lion fell dead almost on the
buffalo ; he had merely time to turn toward us,
seize a bush with his teeth, and drop dead with
the stick in his jaws. The second made off immediately ; and the third raised his head, coolly
looked round for a moment, and then went on
tearing and biting the carcass as hard as ever.
We retired a short distance to load, then again
advanced and fired. The lion made off, but a
ball that he received *ought* to have stopped him,

as it went clean through his shoulder-blade. He was followed up and killed, after having charged several times. Both lions were males. It is not often that one *bags* a brace of lions and a buffalo in about ten minutes. It was an exciting adventure, and I shall never forget it.

"Such, my dear Livingstone, is the plain, unvarnished account. The buffalo had of course gone close to where the lions were lying down for the day; and they, seeing him lame and bleeding, thought the opportunity too good a one to be lost.

"Ever yours,

"FRANK VARDON."

CHAPTER V.

A Curious-Bird's Nest—Crossing the River Chobe—Re-
ception at Linyanti—Journeying with a Chief—A
Fleet of Canoes—The River Leeambye—Summary
Punishment of Treason—Return to Linyanti.

L EAVING the lions and buffaloes of our last
chapter, we will now give attention to our
journey. The country over which it now led to
the North was very beautiful. The grass was
green, and often higher than the wagons. Vines
festooned the trees, among which were the pal-
myro, wild date, the banian, with its drop-shoots,
and others, which were new to our travelers.
Then came water-courses—small rivers twenty
yards wide and four feet deep. They became
broader and deeper as the party moved forward.
Elephants, by wading in them, had made many
deep holes, in which the oxen floundered des-
perately, breaking the pole of a wagon, and compelling Livingstone to work for three hours and a
half in the water up to his breast.

Coming at last to the river Sanshureh, the
company halted under a magnificent mowana-

tree, and began exploring for a ford across the
stream. So many ineffectual attempts were
made to cross the river that the Bushmen became tired of the work. They were kept some
days by presents, but finally slipped off by night.
Livingstone now found he could do no better
than to take one of the strongest of his sick
companions and cross in a pontoon—the gift of
Captains Webb and Codrington. Then taking
with them some provisions and a blanket for
each, they made their way westward for a distance of twenty miles, across a plain covered
with water ankle deep, with thick grass which
reached above the knees. At evening they
came to an immense wall of reeds six or eight
feet high. When they attempted to force their
passage through these reeds the water was found
so deep they were obliged to retreat. They now
thought they had reached the river Chobe, for
which they were looking, and where they hoped
to find some of the Makololo people; so they directed their course to some trees seen at the
South, in order to find a bed and get a view of
the adjacent country.

While gathering wood Livingstone found a
curious bird's-nest, made of live leaves sewed together with threads of the spider's web. It exhibited ingenuity and skill. The threads were

pushed through small punctures, and thickened to a knot. Unfortunately this pretty contrivance was lost. It was the second nest resembling that of the tailor-bird of India which Livstone had seen.

Next morning, by climbing the highest trees, they got a sight of a fine large sheet of water, but surrounded on all sides with the same impenetrable wall of reeds. This proved to be the broad part of the river Chobe, called Zabesa. Two islands, covered with trees, seemed nearer the broad water than the shore on which they stood, and they made an attempt to reach them. The reeds through which they had to pass were mingled with a peculiar serrated grass, which at certain angles cut the hand like a razor. The climbing convolulus, with stalks strong as whipcord, tied the mass together. Struggling to force a passage through this tangled belt, they felt like pigmies. Sometimes the only possible way of progress was by both leaning against a part, and bending it down till they could stand upon it. There was no ventilation among the reeds, and as the sun rose high the heat was stifling, and the perspiration streamed off their bodies. They were in the water up to their knees, and this was refreshing. At last they reached one of the islands, after some hours of severe toil. Here they met an old acquaintance — the bramble-bush. Livingstone's stout moleskins were worn through at the knees, and the leather pantaloons of his companion were torn, and his legs bleeding. Tearing his handkerchief in two pieces, Livingstone tied them around his knees. Now they were met by a new difficulty. Great masses of papyrus, eight or ten feet high, and an inch and a half in diameter, stood before them. These were laced together by convolvulus so strongly as to resist the weight of both of them. At last they found a passage made by a hippopotamus, which let them out into the clear water.

Spending the night in a deserted hut, on a large ant-hill, and the next morning in exploring, they launched their pontoon about midday, and paddled on till sunset, upon the river Chobe. This stream here was deep, and from eighty to one hundred yards wide. All along the wall of reeds lined each bank. Just as the brief evening twilight began, their cheerless prospect of spending the night without supper in the boat was brightened by the sight of a village on the island of Mahonta. It proved to be the village of Moremi, one of Livingstone's Makololo acquaintances, who was now located here. The villagers seemed as much astonished as though

AFRICAN GIRLS.

they had seen a ghost. In their figurative style they said: " He has dropped among us from the clouds, yet came riding upon the back of a hippopotamus. We Makololo thought no one could cross the Chobe without our knowledge, but here he drops among us like a bird."

The next day they returned across the flooded lands in canoes. When they reached the wagons they found the men had allowed the cattle to wander into a small piece of woods infested with the poisonous insect tsetse. By this carelessness ten fine oxen were lost. After a few days, some of the principal Makololo men from Linyanti came down to help them over the river. They took the wagons to pieces, and ferried them across on several canoes lashed together. ·Then they drove the oxen over, swimming and diving among them more like alligators than men. On the 23d of May, 1853, the party reached Linyanti, the capital town of the Makololo.

The population of the town is between six and seven thousand. All came out with eager curiosity to see the wagons in motion — a phenomenon they had never seen before. Their chief, Sekeletu, received the travelers in what was there regarded as princely style. A large number · of pots of boyaloa, or beer, were set before them. Each of the women who brought them took a drink to show there was no poison. Soon after his arrival at Linyanti, Sekeletu took Livingstone aside and urged him to mention those things he liked best, and wished to get from him. Any thing, either in his town or out of it, he said would be freely given, only let it be named. Livingstone told him his purpose was to teach him and his people, and lead them to become Christians. But the chief replied he did not wish to learn to read the Book for fear "it might change his heart, and make him content with one wife, like Sechele." Livingstone assured him the change of heart would make him just as happy and contented with one wife as he was now with several, and that the whole matter would be left to his own voluntary decision. " No, no," said he, " I want always to have five wives at least."

The Makololo women work but little. Their families are spread over the country as the lords of the land, one or two in each village. They exercise lordship over numbers of subjugated tribes, who are called Makololo. Their serfs render service of certain kinds to their conquerors, aiding in the cultivation of their fields. But the serfdom is very mild, since any one unkindly treated can easily escape to other tribes. For the most part they are treated more like children than slaves.

No fugitive-slave law can be enforced, and a Makololo master, whose ill treatment of his servants forfeits their affections, is likely to find himself left some morning without a single servant. The servants have their own land for cultivation, and live quite independently.

The ladies of the Makololo drink large quantities of boyaloa, which is very nutritious, and gives them a plumpness which they consider beautiful. They do not like being seen by persons of the other sex when at their potations. Their beer is made of the grain called durasaifi, or holcus sorghum. It is similar to the birsa of the Arabs. These ladies cut their woolly hair quite short, and delight in having their persons shining with butter. For their dress they wear a garment made of oxhide, so dressed as to be soft as cloth. It reaches to the knees, and is not ungraceful. When unemployed, a soft skin mantle, thrown across the shoulders, is added to complete the dress of the lady. For ornaments they wear heavy brass anklets, and bracelets both of brass and ivory. Sometimes the heavy rings on the ankles produce blisters, but this is patiently borne for the sake of fashion. Strings of beads are hung around the neck. For these the fashionable colors are light-green and pink. The religious services were announced by the herald, and were often attended by five to seven hundred persons. The people behaved with decorum, except at the conclusion of prayer. When they kneeled down, those who had children bent over the little ones. In fear of being crushed, the children would set up a simultaneous cry. This excited a suppressed titter among the women, which burst out in a hearty laugh soon as the amen was spoken.

Livingstone's looking-glass was a matter of great curiosity to these people. Their remarks elicited by the first sight of their own features were often quite laughable. They were such as these: "My ears are big as pumpkin leaves." "What a big mouth I have!" "I would have been pretty, but am spoiled by those high cheek-bones." One man, who came alone, to gaze in quiet at his own features, very honestly said to himself, "People say I am ugly, and how very ugly I am indeed!"

The Makololo make shields as well as mantles of the hides of oxen. These are partially dried in the sun, and then beaten with hammers till dry and stiff. Two broad belts of skin, differently colored, are sewed into them lengthwise. Sticks, too, are inserted to keep them from becoming pliable. They afford great protection from spears and javelins. They are quite skillful in the use of their spears. When they have room to run a little distance they can throw them forty or fifty yards. Livingstone saw a man who had received one in battle in the shin. When the battle was over, the blade was found to have split the bone, and was driven in with such force that it became necessary to press the split bone asunder with an ax, in order to get the weapon out.

While at Linyanti, on the 23d of May, Livingstone had his first attack of the prevalent fever of the country. Hoping to find some more potent remedy than his own medicines, he requested the aid of one of the chief doctors. But after being stewed in vapor baths, and smoked, and charmed, he came to the conclusion he could cure the fever quicker than they.

The Makololo made a garden and planted maize for the missionary. The corn is pounded into fine meal in large wooden mortars. Sekeletu supplied him with ten or twelve jars of honey of about two gallons each, and an ox every week or two. The hospitable chief furnished milk from two cows appropriated to the use of the traveler. It is the custom of the country for the chief thus to entertain strangers who come on business with him, and take up their abode in his kotla. When strangers have acquaintance with the under chiefs, as is frequently the case, they turn aside to their kotlas, and are entertained in a like manner.

These people cultivate a large extent of land around their villages, on which they raise holcus, sorghum beans, ground-nuts, pumpkins, watermelons, and cucumbers. In other parts of the country sugar-cane, the sweet potato, and manioc are added to the list of agricultural products. The hoe is the implement of tillage through all this country.

Sekeletu receives tribute from a large number of tribes in corn, ground-nuts, spears, hoes, canoes, paddles, wooden vessels, honey, tobacco, dried fruits, prepared skins, and ivory. These things he divides among the crowd of loungers who gather about his kotla, reserving only a small portion for himself. If he is not more liberal to others than himself, he loses popularity. Instances sometimes occur in which a person who feels aggrieved, runs away to other chiefs.

One of this class, who fled to Lechulatebe, was encouraged by that chief to go to a village on the river Chobe and take the tribute which belonged to Sekeletu. This enraged the whole of the Makololo. Some of Lechulatebe's people having come on a visit to Linyanti, a public demonstration was made. About five hundred armed Makololo went through a mimic fight. The principal warriors pointed their spears toward the lake, where Lechulatebe lives; and every thrust in that direction was answered with the simultaneous shout from the whole company, "Hoo!" At every stab on the ground all yelled out, "Huzz!"

On such occasions all capable of bearing arms are required to muster at the call. In Sebituane's time, any one remaining in the house was hunted and killed without mercy.

Lechulatebe repeated his offense, and added to it by permitting a song to be sung in his town, as an accompaniment to the dances, expressing joy at the death of Sebituane. That great chief had enjoined upon his people to live in peace with those at the lake. Sekeletu felt disposed to adopt this advice as his rule of action. But Lechulatebe, having got possession of fire-arms, thought himself fully able to cope with the Makololo. His people had been deprived of some cattle by Sebituane. And as forgiveness does not take high rank among the virtues with these tribes, he thought he had a right to make reprisals if he could. It is a very difficult thing to make these people feel the wickedness of shedding human blood. Accustomed to it from infancy, they are callous to the enormity of the crime.

Livingstone, however, used all his influence with the Makololo to persuade them that if they wished to enjoy peace they must allow others to do so. At the same time he sent a message to

Lechulatebe, advising that he give up the course
he had been following, and especially the song,
because though the great chief, Sebituane, was
dead, the arms with which he fought were still alive
and strong.   In obedience to the instructions of his
father, and for the sake of promoting peace, Sekeletu sent ten cows to Lechulatebe to be exchanged
for sheep.   The party who went with the cows
took hoes with which to purchase goats.   In accordance with the relative value of these animals,
Lechulatebe ought to have sent six sheep for each
cow, but he returned only ten.   One of Sekeletu's
men was found trying to trade his hoes with the
people of a village, without formal permission
from Lechulatebe.   And this chief punished him
by compelling him to sit some hours on the broil-
ing hot sand—at least 130°.   This completed the
breach of amicable relations between the two
tribes.   However, Livingstone's great influence
with the Makololo prevented their going to war
with that tribe of Bechuanas, which had given
them so much offense, and for which they mani-
festly felt a supreme contempt.

   When Livingstone took his departure from Linyanti, he was accompanied to the Barotse country
by Sekeletu and about one hundred and sixty
attendants, consisting of young men, and several
under-chiefs.   The country over which they passed

was perfectly flat, with the exception of occasional patches elevated a few feet above the general level, and the numerous mounds on which gigantic ant-hills were, or had been situated. The industry of the little workers, who build these little structures, is marvelous. The Makololo find the ant-hills choice spots for growing early corn, or any thing on which they wish to bestow especial care. The soil seems to have fertility imparted to it by passing through the mouths of the ants. In this part of the country, these mounds were covered with date-trees, which bear a small fruit. The Makololo, having abundance of food, take no pains to preserve the wild fruit-trees, and so whenever a date-tree is filled with fruit, they cut it down, to save the trouble of climbing to gather the dates.

This company of travelers constituted rather a romantic-looking caravan. The long line of Makololo attendants wound along the meandering foot-path, now and then partially hidden from view, behind the mounds, with the ostrich feathers of their caps waving in the wind. Some of the men had the white ends of oxtails for plumes, instead of ostrich feathers, and some caps were made of lion's manes. Some wore red tunics. Some had tunics of various colored prints, which the chief had bought of Fleming, the colored trader.　The common men carried burdens.　The gentlemen walked with a small club of rhinoceros horn in their hands, accompanied by servants, who carried their shields.　The Machaka, or battle-ax men, carried their own shields and weapons, and were liable to be sent off at any time on an errand a hundred miles away, when they would be expected to run all the way.　Sekeletu is always attended by his own mopato, or body-guard, consisting of a number of young men of his own age.　When he sits down they crowd around him.　Those nearest eat out of his dish.　The Makololo chiefs pride themselves on eating with their people.　The chief eats a little, then beckons his neighbors to partake.　When they have done so, he may beckon some one at a distance to share in the mess.　The person thus invited immediately comes forward, takes the pot and removes it to his own companions.

Sekeletu rode on Livingstone's horse, and his comrades, wishing to imitate him, leaped on the backs of some half-broken Batoka oxen.　But having no saddles or bridles they were very frequently tumbled off, to the great amusement of the rest of the party.　Herds of "lechwes" — a species of water antelopes—were feeding carelessly all over these flats.

Whenever a village was reached in the journey,

the women all gathered to welcome their chief. By a rapid motion of the tongue they make their shrill voices tremulous, while they shout, "Great Lion," "Great Chief," "Sleep my Lord," etc. The men give similar salutations, all of which Sekeletu received with dignified indifference. After conversation of a few minutes, during which the news is related, the head man of the village, nearly always a Makololo, rises and brings forth a number of large pots of beer. Calabashes are used as drinking cups, and as many as can partake of the beverage, clutching the drinking cups so eagerly that they are in danger of being broken. Large bowls of thick milk are also presented to the company. These bowls sometimes contain six or eight gallons. They, as well as the pots of beer, are each given to a particular person, who may divide them as he pleases. Spoons are not in fashion, and the milk is conveyed to the mouth by the hand. Livingstone sometimes presented his friends with spoons. They were delighted with them, but still ate with the hand, dipping with the spoon into the left hand, and eating out of that.

The Makololo have abundance of cattle. The chief has cattle stations all over the country. From these he selects an ox or two, to feed those who accompany him. Or he may be supplied by way of tribute by the head men of the villages he visits. The cattle are killed by a small javelin thrust into the region of the heart. The object of the butcher is to shed as little blood as possible, as this with the internal parts of the animal belong to him. For this reason all are eager to render service of this kind. Each tribe has its own way of cutting up and distributing an animal. Among the Bakwains the breast belongs to the chief. Among the Makololo the hump and ribs are his perquisites. After the oxen are cut up, the different joints are placed before the chief, and he distributes them among the gentlemen of the party. The whole is very quickly divided among their attendants, and by them cut into long strips, and thrown upon the fire. Half broiled, and burning hot, the meat is handed round. They do not aim at any enjoyment in eating, but to get as much as possible into the stomach, while the rest are cramming themselves. No one is allowed to eat after the others have finished. So no one gets a chance to masticate his food but the chief. They despise any one who eats alone. So Livingstone, at his meals, always poured out two cups of coffee—of which he had a good supply—and invited the chief or some one of the principal men to share with him. They all soon became very fond of this beverage. Sekeletu relished it very much, and said, "I know your heart loves me, because I find my own heart warming to your food." He had been visited by some traders and Griquas, during Livingstone's absence at the Cape. "Their coffee," he said, "did not taste half so nice, because they loved his ivory, and not himself"—a novel and original method of discriminating characters.

Livingstone and Sekeletu had each a little gipsy tent in which to sleep. But in some of the villages the mice disturbed his sleep by running over his face; or hungry dogs prowling around ate up his shoes, leaving nothing but the soles. Then he got the loan of a hut for protection from these annoyances. The best of the Makololo huts are made with three circular walls, with small holes for doors, like that of a dog-house, through which you must creep on all-fours, bending down the body at that. The roof is made of reeds and straight sticks, bound firmly together with circular bands, which are secured with the strong inner bark of the mamosa-tree. In shape it is like a Chinaman's hat. Over all is a thatch-work of fine grass, sewed together with the bark just mentioned. This projects beyond the walls, and reaches within four feet of the ground. These huts are very cool in the hottest days, but at night are close and defective in ventilation. The huts of the Makaloka are infested with vermin. But

those of the Makololo are kept clean by frequently
smearing the floors with a plaster made of earth
and the droppings of the cattle. The bed is a
mat of rushes sewed together with twine. When
game was wanted, Livingstone did the hunting,
because the Makololo wasted his powder with
bad shooting. On one occasion he shot a beautiful cow-eland, which he found standing in the
shade of a fine tree. She had evidently just lost
her calf by the voracity of a lion. On her hind-
quarters were long, deep scratches, as if she had
been attacked herself, the lion failing to pull her
down. When lying on the ground the milk
flowed from the large udder. It was a new unde-
scribed variety of this beautiful antelope. It was
marked with narrow, white bands across the body,
and a black spot of more than a handbreadth on
the outer side of the forearm. Lebeole, a Makololo gentleman, who accompanied the missionary
on this hunt, speaking of the beauty and size of
the splendid animal just shot, said, " Jesus ought
to have given us these instead of cattle."

After some delay in gathering canoes, our large
company of travelers began to ascend the river
Leeambye. Livingstone had his choice of the
whole fleet, and selected a canoe thirty-four feet
long by twenty inches wide. It was not the largest, but the best. He had six paddlers, while the

larger canoe of Sekeletu had ten. They stand erect and keep stroke with great precision, changing from side to side as the direction they wished to go may demand. The strongest and most expert men stand at the head and stern. The canoes are flat-bottomed, and will float in very shallow water. The paddles are about eight feet long, and are used as poles to push the boats when they strike shallow water. The fleet consisted of thirty-three canoes, manned by about one hundred and sixty men. Skimming along so rapidly, the paddlers keeping time so admirably, it was a beautiful sight. The relation of the Makololo and Makaloka is changed somewhat when they are on the water. Here the latter are more independent. They fear their masters less, and can not be prevented from racing with each other; sometimes dashing along at such a rate as to endanger the lives of their lords. Should a canoe capsize many of the Makololo would go to the bottom like stones. On the day the fleet started a case of this kind occurred. The wind blowing strongly from the east raised large waves on the river. An old Makololo doctor had his canoe filled with water, and being unable to swim, was drowned. The Barotse who were in the canoe swam to the shore, and were saved. They were afraid of being punished with death for not saving the doctor. Had he been a man of considerable influence their fears would undoubtedly have been realized. The fleet proceeded rapidly up the river, a magnificent stream, more than a mile wide in many places. The banks are lined with forest; most of the trees nearest the edge of the water sending down roots from their branches, like the banian or *Ficus Indica*—the numerous islands so densely covered with forest, that at a little distance they "seem great rounded masses of silvan vegetation reclining on the bosom of the glorious stream." The beauty of the scenery of some of the islands is greatly increased by the date-palm, with its gracefully curved fronds and refreshing light-green color, near the bottom of the picture, and the lofty palmyra towering far above, and casting its feathery foliage against a cloudless sky. "It being Winter, we had the strange coloring on the banks which many parts of African landscape assume." Many villages of the Banyeti, a poor and industrious people, are seen dotting the shores. Livingstone felt great pleasure in looking upon scenery so beautiful, which had never been looked upon before by a European. The soil is of a reddish color; and very fertile, as is shown by the large quantities of grain raised by the inhabitants of these villages. They are skillful hunters of the hippopotamus and other game;

and manufacture many articles of wood and iron, with a great deal of taste and skill. Some make large wooden vessels with neat lids, and wooden bowls of various sizes. And since the Makololo have adopted the fashion of sitting on stools, these Banyeti have shown much ingenuity in the varied forms given to the legs of these pieces of furniture. This whole country is infested with the tsetse, so that domestic animals can not be kept. Perhaps this may account in part for the skill in handicraft exhibited by its inhabitants. Other of these tribes excel in the manufacture of iron and pottery, while others make neat and strong baskets from the split roots of trees. They have never been warlike.

In the center of the country, out of the range of the slave-trade, there have very seldom been wars involving any other questions than the possession of cattle. Some tribes even refuse to keep cattle simply on this ground. Livingstone tells us he has heard of but one war originating in any other cause. Three brothers among the Barolongs went to battle, and fought for the possession of a woman. And the quarrel resulted in the permanent division of the tribe.

As they passed up the river, the inhabitants of the different villages came out to present their tribute to Sekeletu, in the form of food and skins.

At Gonye, where there is a large village of Banyeti, the river falls about thirty feet. The water
of the stream, before making the leap, is narrowed
to the space of seventy or eighty yards ; and thus
the roar of the cataract is very loud. Here they
were obliged to take the canoes out of the water,
and carry them for a mile up the stream. In
this task the people of Gonye were required to
assist.

The Barotse valley, as it is called, through
which this river runs, has a very close resem-
blance to the valley of the Nile. It is annually
inundated by the overflow of the river Leeambye,
just as lower Egypt is flooded by the Nile. The
villages are built on mounds, some of which are
said to have been raised artificially by a former
chief. During the annual inundation the whole
valley appears like a large lake, with the villages
for islands. The valley is very fertile. One species of grass was seen twelve feet high, with a
stem as thick as a man's thumb. The immense
herds of cattle kept by the Makololo never eat off
the pasturage. This was Sekeletu's first visit to
this part of the country since his elevation to the
chieftainship. Those who had taken part with
Mpepe, who had set up a claim to that position,
were now in very great terror.

When they came to the town of Mpepe's father,

as he and another man had advised the killing of
Sekeletu, they were taken and tossed into the
river. When Livingstone remonstrated against
this off-hand way of taking human life, the counselors justified their act by the evidence in the
case, and calmly added, "You see we are still
Boers; we are not yet taught."

Naliele, the capital of the Barotse, is built on
a mound, constructed by an ancient chief, Santuru. This was his store-house for grain, while
his own capital stood about five hundred yards
south, where is now the bed of the river. The
same thing has happened to the sites of other
towns. This chief, at whose ancient granary
our company are resting, was a famous hunter,
and fond of taming wild animals. Some of his
people, it is said, who were accustomed to bring
him every young antelope they could catch, captured on one occasion two young hippopotami,
which they presented to him. These animals
gamboled in the river by day, but never failed to
come up at night for their suppers of milk and
meal. They were the wonder of the country,
till a stranger, who came to visit Santuru, saw
them reclining in the sun, and speared one of
them, thinking they were wild. A like misfor-
tune happened in Livingstone's case. He had
brought a pair of cats to Sekeletu. A stranger,

seeing an animal new to himself, killed it, and brought the trophy to the chief, thinking he had made a wonderful discovery.

Satisfied by this exploration that no healthy location could be found for a mission station where the Makololo could live in peace, Livingstone returned to Linyanti, after a tour of nine weeks. He had been, during this time, in closer contact with heathenism than ever before. And this produced, as he tells us, a more intense disgust for it, and a higher appreciation of the indirect benefits or latent effects of missions. These savage men, from the chief to the poorest of them, were all very kind to him, "yet," he says, "to endure the dancing, roaring, and singing, the jesting, anecdotes, grumbling, quarreling, and murdering of these children of nature, seemed more like a severe penance than any thing I had before met with in the course of my missionary duties."

CHAPTER VI.

A PICHO—VOYAGING ON THE RIVER—ALLIGATORS AND THEIR
EGGS—A FEMALE CHIEF—GRAND RECEPTION—A MAGIC
LANTERN AT COURT.

L IVINGSTONE now began preparations for
a journey to Loanda. And as the Makololo
were desirous to open a trade directly with the
sea-coast, he proposed to them to join in the
expedition. A "picho" or public meeting was
called, to deliberate upon the matter. The largest liberty of speech is allowed in these assem-
blies. And on this occasion an old diviner, famous for being a croaker, such as may be found
in other parts of the world, said, "Where is he
taking you to? This white man is throwing you
away. Your garments already smell of blood."
Sekeletu laughed at him, and the general voice
was in favor of the missionary's plan. A band
of twenty-seven men was appointed to accompany
him to the west. The three men he had brought
from Kuruman had frequent relapses of fever,
and required waiting upon instead of rendering
any service ; so he determined to send them south

10

with Fleming, whenever he should finish his trading so as to return. Livingstone himself was debilitated by the fever he had suffered. A strange giddiness affected him. Whenever he looked up suddenly toward the sky every thing seemed whirling to the left. And if he did not save himself by catching hold of some object he fell heavily to the ground.

The Makololo now put the question to him, "In the event of your death will not the white people blame us for having allowed you to go away into an unhealthy, unknown country of enemies?" He told them·he would leave a book with Sekeletu to be sent to Mr. Moffat in case he did not return, which would explain the whole matter, and free them from blame.

This book was a volume of his journal, which, with a letter to Mr. Moffat, Sekeletu delivered to a trader, when Livingstone was detained longer than he expected. But he never heard of it afterward. This was matter of much regret, as it contained many valuable notes on the habits of wild animals, with other matters of interest. His own feelings, in view of the possibility of death in that barbarous land, are thus expressed: "The prospect of passing away from this fair and beautiful world thus came before me in a pretty plain, matter-of-fact form, and it did seem a serious thing to leave wife and children—to break up all connection with earth, and enter on an untried state of existence; and I find myself in my journal pondering over that fearful migration which lands us in eternity, wondering whether an angel will soothe the fluttering soul, sadly flurried as it must be on entering the spirit-world, and hoping that Jesus might speak one word of peace, for that would establish in the bosom an everlasting calm. But as I had always believed that if we serve God at all it ought to be done in a manly way, I wrote to my brother, commending our little girl to his care, as I was determined to 'succeed or perish in the attempt to open up this part of Africa.' The Boers, by taking possession of all my goods, had saved me the trouble of making a will; and considering the light heart now left in my bosom, and some faint efforts to perform the Christian charity of forgiveness, I felt it was better to be the plundered party than one of the plunderers."

Livingstone had found that the secret of successful travel lay in having as few impediments as possible. Hence the outfit for this journey was very spare. It consisted of a few biscuits, a few pounds of tea and sugar, about twenty pounds of coffee, a cannister of medicines, a nautical almanac, Thompson's Logarithms, a Bible, a few good scientific instruments, a gipsy tent just large enough to sleep in, a sheep-skin mantle, a house-rug for a bed, a magic lantern, three muskets for the men, a rifle and double-barreled smooth-bore for Livingstone, and a scanty wardrobe to be used when they reached civilized life. With this equipment they left Linyanti, to embark on the river Chobe. Sekeletu and his principal men accompanied the travelers to the river, to see that every thing was right at the start. The chief lent his own canoe to Livingstone. The river is much infested with hippopotami. They are not dangerous except when a canoe comes into the midst of a herd when they are all asleep. Then in their fright they may strike a canoe and break it in pieces. Occasionally, too, elderly males are driven out from the herd by the rest, and compelled to live alone. These solitary "old bachelors" very naturally acquire a morose temper, which prompts them to attack every canoe that passes near them. In case of such an attack, the canoe being wrecked, the natives dive to the bottom of the river, holding themselves down a few seconds. The hippopotamus looks on the surface of the water for the occupants of the boat he has smashed, and not seeing them, soon moves off. Then the submerged men rise to the surface and make their escape. Having left the Chobe, our travelers ascended the Leeambye, and on the 19th of November reached the town of Sesheke. The town is composed of parties of various tribes. But the Makololo rule over them all. There is a large population of Makalaka. Mori-antsane, a brother-in-law of Sebituane, is the ruling chief. His rule is mainly despotic. Yet it is modified by certain laws and customs. A culprit, who had speared an ox belonging to one of the Makololo, being unable to extract the spear, was thereby caught. He was bound hand and foot in the burning sun, to force him to pay a fine. He, however, persisted in denying his guilt. At last his mother, believing him innocent, came forward, and with her hoe in hand, threatened to cut down any one who should interfere. She then unbound him, and took him home. The chief did not punish this resistance to his authority, but referred it to Sekeletu, at Linyanti.

A stranger having come to this village on a trading expedition, most of his goods were stolen by one of the Makaloka. When caught he confessed the theft. The Makololo gentlemen were greatly enraged at the thought of having the reputation of their village stained by such treatment of a stranger. Their customary mode of punishment had been to throw the criminal into the river. But this would not restore the lost property.

So they referred the case to Livingstone. He
solved the difficulty by paying for the goods
from his own pocket, and sentencing the thief to
work out an equivalent with his hoe in a garden.
This method of punishment was at once adopted
by the natives, and thieves are now condemned
to raise an amount of corn proportioned to their
crimes. A Bakwain woman, who had stolen from
the garden of another, was compelled to give her
own garden to the person she had injured.

These people have no regular day of rest, except the day after the first appearance of the
new moon. Then they only refrain from going
to their gardens. They watch with intense eagerness for the earliest glimpse of the new moon, and
when, after the sun has set, they catch the faint
outline of the pale orb of night, they utter a loud
shout, "Kna," and vociferate prayers to the moon.
Livingstone's men, on this occasion, shouted,
"Let our journey with the white man be pros-
perous! Let our enemies perish, and the children of Nake become rich! May he have plenty
of meat on this journey!"

Livingstone made frequent public addresses to
the people of Sesheke, under the outspread
branches of a camelthorn-tree, on the river's
bank. The sight was pleasant as the men, women, and children came out from different parts

of the town, winding their way in long lines, each party led by its head man. They often numbered five or six hundred persons, who were gathered in this native temple to listen to the missionary. For the most part they were very attentive. On one occasion Moriantsane, the chief, thinking to please the missionary, hurled his staff at the heads of some young fellows who, instead of listening, were improving the time in working at a skin of some kind they were dressing.

Sometimes the hearers would ask the most sensible questions, and at other times they would turn immediately from listening to the most solemn truths and introduce the most frivolous nonsense. Some begin in secret to pray as soon as they hear of the white man's God, and, though they have very imperfect notions of what they are doing or the proper method of prayer, they are doubtless heard by that merciful God who would have all men feel after him and find him, and who pitieth all who fear him like as a father pitieth his children.

Passing through a beautiful country, the travelers reached Gonye Falls the 30th of November, 1853. They were much wearied with travel. The weather was extremely hot, and the season so dry that, though the trees were robed in their

gayest dress, and numerous flowers were blooming, yet the midday sun caused all the leaves to
droop and the whole landscape to look languid
for want of rain.

Would you like to know a little more in de-
tail the method of proceeding on this journey?
Then take one day as a specimen of the rest.
Just at the dawn of day—a little before five
o'clock—the company rise. While the missionary is at his morning toilet coffee is prepared.
While he and the principal men are sipping their
coffee the servants are busy loading the canoes,
and immediately they embark for the day's sail.
These morning hours are the most pleasant of
the whole day, and the stout, broad-shouldered
Barotse boatmen paddle swiftly along. About
eleven o'clock the party land, and make their
dinner from any meat that has remained from
the supper of the previous night, or, if not so
fortunate, they eat biscuit with honey, and drink
water. An hour of rest, and they launch away
upon the river again. Livingstone seeks some
slight protection from the burning rays of the
sun by cowering under an umbrella. The men,
exposed to the intense heat while they toil at the
paddles, perspire profusely, and in the afternoon
grow faint and languid. All are glad to stop two
hours before sunset, if a suitable place can be

found. Again they refresh themselves with coffee. Biscuit, or coarse bread of Indian meal, or that of the native corn make up the bill of fare. If they have been fortunate enough to kill game during the day, the meat is cut up in long strips, placed in a kettle, and water poured on it in sufficient quantity to cover it. When it is boiled nearly dry the dish is ready.

Next comes the work of preparation for the night's lodging. Mashuana, the head boatman, plants the poles of the little tent. These poles are used during the day for carrying burdens, as occasion may require. A bed is made of grass, with boxes placed along each side, and the tent spread over the whole. A few feet in front of this tent, which is Livingstone's sleeping apartment, is the kotla fire. The wood for this fire is gathered by the man who holds the position of herald, who claims the heads of all the game and oxen killed by the party as the perquisites of his office. The head boatman makes his bed at the door of the tent. While sleeping or waking, the two Makololo men place themselves at the right and left of the missionary. The servants divide into small companies, according to their tribes, and build sheds around the fire. These sheds are built with poles resting on forked posts to form the front. Branches of trees are stuck in

the ground in an inclined position, and the twigs
tied with bark to the horizontal pole. The front
of the shed is toward the fire. The roof is covered with long grass. A large horseshoe shaped
space is left in front for the cattle to stand in.
In less than an hour after the preparations begin
they are usually all under cover. Except when
the moon shines very brightly, the fire is a necessary protection against wild animals. Even
the oxen understand this, and are less easily
frightened when in sight of the fire.

The people of the villages through which our
missionary passed on this journey were, for the
most part, exceedingly kind and generous in
their conduct toward him. They gave him liberal supplies of butter, milk, and meal, with occasionally the present of an ox. They presented
these gifts very gracefully. When an ox was
given the generous donor would say, "Here is a
little bit of bread for you."

•Part of the company marched along the banks
with the oxen, and a part were in the canoes,
the speed of travel being governed by the men
on shore. Their task was sometimes hard and
difficult, because they were often obliged to cross
the numerous streams flowing into the Leeambye
River. The alligators were much too plenty in
these streams for the safety of the men, who

were frequently under the necessity of swimming them. One of these swimmers was one day caught by an alligator and dragged to the bottom. But his presence of mind did not forsake him even then. Having with him a small javelin with a ragged edge, he gave his new acquaintance an unwelcome stab behind the shoulder, which sent him away writhing in pain. Released from the grasp of his enemy, the man came out, with deep marks of the ugly reptile's teeth on his thigh.

Among the Bakwain and Bamangwato tribes such an accident would have worse consequences than among these people. There, if one is bitten by an alligator, or even has bad water splashed over him by the reptile's tail, he is expelled from his tribe. They eat the flesh of the zebra without any reluctance; yet, if a man is bitten by one, he is expelled from the tribe, and compelled to take away his family to the Kalahari. These are curious relics of the animal worship of former times, which have scarcely any existence among the Makololo.

Along the Barotse Valley, through which our travelers passed, they saw great numbers of large black geese. There were, too, myriads of ducks, of two varieties. Livingstone's canoe came one day near a bank where a large flock were sitting.

Two shots were fired, and seventeen ducks and a goose were picked up as the result. Thus the whole party were furnished with a full supply of game for supper. On some parts of the journey they met enormous herds of antelopes, and other game. Flocks of green pigeons and many new kinds of birds were seen. On one of the Sabbaths spent during this expedition Livingstone's men, who wandered about after morning worship, brought him several varieties of wild fruit he had not seen before. One called mogametsa is a kind of bean, with a small quantity of pulp around it which tastes like sponge cake. Another kind, which grows in great abundance on a low bush, is called mawa. Many of these fruits our traveler thinks might, with careful culture, take high rank among the fruits of the world.

On the 27th of December our party reached the confluence of the Leeba and Leeambye Rivers. After some delay in arrangements for the return of captives who had been taken from different tribes by their enemies, and whom Livingstone had succeeded in rescuing, the travelers left the main stream and began the ascent of the Leeba. This river flows calmly and slowly through charming meadows, each one of which has a soft, sedgy center, a large pond, or a rill trickling through the middle. Numerous little streamlets come pouring in their tributary waters on either side. The trees on the banks are planted in groups with a gracefulness and beauty which no human art could excel. They are covered with a fresh, luxuriant foliage. Beautiful flowers are blooming, while busy bees, in large numbers, sip their nectar. Plenty of honey is found in the woods.

One tree in bloom brought back to the missionary's recollection the fragrance of English hawthorn hedges. The leaves, fragrance, flowers, and fruit "resembled those of the hawthorn, only the flowers were as large as dog-roses, and the 'haws' like boys' marbles."

The next night after reaching the mouth of the Leeba our party of travelers built their fire in a deserted alligator's nest. Broken shells were strewed all around. The eggs of the alligator are about the size of those of a goose, but are of equal diameter at both ends. Livingstone tells us he has seen sixty of them taken from one nest. A broad path led up from the water's edge to the nest, a distance of about ten feet. There were indications that this same place had been used for several previous years. When the alligator leaves her nest after filling it with eggs, she covers them with about four inches of earth.

No further attention is needed till the proper time for the brood to hatch. Then she returns and aids the young in getting out of shell and nest. She then leads them to the edge of the water, and leaves the family to catch fish for themselves. The yolk of these eggs is eaten by the natives. The young which had lately come out of these nests were not very shy. They were about ten inches long, with yellow eyes, and pale green and brown stripes, half an inch wide, across the body. When speared they uttered a sharp bark, like that of a young pup, and bit the spear very fiercely. Fish constitute the principal food of the alligator. In this part of Africa they are more savage and do more mischief than elsewhere. Young men who run down to the river to refresh themselves by bathing, after a long dance in the moonlight, are sometimes caught by these reptiles and carried off. Yet their comrades repeat the night bathing, and seem to have no fear. If they escape from an encounter of this kind, they only laugh afterward at the circumstance. They are too thoughtless to be troubled with fear.

About the first of January the rainy season set in, with heavy rains almost every day. For two weeks the sky was so constantly covered with clouds that Livingstone was unable to get a single observation for determining latitude or longitude.

Our travelers now reached the village of the female chief Nyamoána, said to be a sister of Kabompo, or Shinte, the greatest chief of the Balonda in this part of the country. When the travelers approached, this lady chief and her husband, Samoána, were sitting on skins placed in the middle of a circle raised a little above the level of the ground, about thirty paces in diameter, and having a trench around it. The husband was clothed in a red and green baize kilt, and armed with a spear and an antique broad-sword eighteen inches long and three in width. Outside the trench sat about a hundred persons of both sexes and all ages. The men were armed with spears, bows, arrows, and broad-swords. Livingstone and his men put down their arms about forty yards away, and he walked up to the middle of the circular bench and saluted Samoána, according to the fashion of the country, by clapping his hands. He, however, pointed to his wife, to indicate that the honor belonged to her. She was then saluted in the same way, and, a mat having been brought, Livingstone seated himself in front of them.

A talker was now called, and Livingstone, being asked who should speak for him, pointed to

his man Kolimbota, who knew their dialect best.
The palaver now began in due form. Kolimbota
delivered to Nyamoána's talker what Livingstone
said, he repeated it verbatim to her husband, and
he to the chief herself. The reply came back
from the lady in the same roundabout way.
After a full and frank statement of the views
and objects of the missionary, and repeated explanations, the palaver came to a close.

Straight hair is a great curiosity among these
people, and, as a means of gaining their confidence, Livingstone showed them his hair. "Is
that hair?" said they. "It is the mane of a lion,
and not hair at all"—and some of them thought
he had made a wig of a lion's mane.

Here the missionary found the first evidence
of idolatry he had seen. It was an old idol left
in a deserted village—simply a human head
carved on a block of wood. When they have
no professional carver, a crooked stick answers
the same purpose, and becomes an idol. These
people are more superstitious than any Dr. Livingstone had before met.

The missionary traveler was anxious to proceed further up the Leeba with the canoes, but
Nyamoána wished her people to conduct him to
her brother Shinte. To the arguments in favor
of traveling by water she replied that her brother

did not live near the river, and there was a cataract a little further up the river over which it
would be difficult to convey the canoes. She
was afraid, too, that the Balobale, being ignorant
of the objects of the travelers, would kill them,
or, if they did not harm Livingstone, would sacrifice his Makololo attendants as enemies to their
tribe. This argument convinced his companions
of the propriety of Nyamoána's plan.

Just at this time the arrival of Manenko—another female chief, and a niece of Shinte—threw
so much weight into the scale in their favor that
Livingstone thought best to yield.

Manenko was a large, tall woman, about twenty
years of age, with a great profusion of ornaments
and medicine charms hung about her person.
Her body was smeared all over with a mixture
of red ocher and fat as a protection against the
weather. This became necessary from her most
frightful nakedness. It was not, however, from
any inability to clothe herself, since, being a
chief, she could have been clad as well as any of
her subjects. But this was the fashion of the
Balonda ladies, and suited her ideas of elegance.
She was attended by her husband, Sambanza,
who acted as her spokesman. They listened for
some time to the statements of the missionary.
Then Sambanza began an oration giving the

reasons of the chief for coming. During his speech he picked up a little sand every two or three seconds and rubbed it on the upper part of his chest and arms. This is a common method of salutation in Londa. When the oration was ended he rose up and showed the bundles of copper rings with which his ankles were decorated. Some chiefs wear so many of them that they are forced to keep one foot apart from the other, and adopt a straggling gait. And this is imitated by gentlemen like Sambanza. He strutted along as if his few ounces of ornaments were double as many pounds. When Livingstone smiled at this folly the people said, "That is the way in which they show off their lordship in these parts."

Our travelers moved on toward the town of Shinte under the conduct of Manenko, who led the march at a rate of speed which few of the men could maintain. Livingstone, being on ox-back, was able to keep up with her; and, as the rain came pouring down upon them incessantly, he took occasion to ask her why she did not clothe herself during the rain. In reply she told him that it was thought improper for a chief, male or female, to appear effeminate. He or she must maintain the appearance of hardy and robust youth. Every now and then the men

remarked, in admiration of her pedestrian powers, "Manenko is a soldier;" and all, being wet
and cold, were glad when she called a halt for
the night.

The country through which they were passing
was covered with evergreen forests, interspersed
with open lawns, on which were luxuriant crops
of grass.

Numerous villages and hamlets were passed
on this journey. It was common to see near
each of them an idol, made of clay and grass, in
the form of an alligator. Yet it is called a lion.
Shells are inserted to form the eyes, and bristles
from the tail of an elephant are stuck on the
neck. It stood in a shed. And in cases of sickness the Balonda beat drums and pray before it
all night. Some of the villages were found deserted, the inhabitants having been seized with
sudden panic. Manenko's drummer beat his
drum the greater part of the time to announce
the coming of great people. When our traveling party remained all night at a village the people kindly lent them the roofs of their own huts.
They are shaped like a Chinaman's hat, and can
be readily lifted off the wall. They were brought
to the spot selected by the travelers for lodging,
and propped up with stakes. Then they were
safely housed for the night.

The party were delayed among some Balonda villages a little south of the town of Shinte, that Manenko might send messengers to inform her uncle of their approach. Livingstone asked why this was necessary, since, according to the belief of the country, the idols of the chief might give the information. The reply was, "she did it only," a form of expression which means she did it without any particular reason. Our missionary remarks in connection with this incident, "It is seldom of much use to show one who worships idols the folly of idolatry without giving something else as an object of adoration instead. They do not love them; they fear them, and betake themselves to their idols only when in perplexity and danger."

Livingstone was suffering with fever, and was much annoyed by this delay; and, as he felt sure the reply from Shinte would be favorable, and this was Saturday, he urged that the party should go forward, so as to spend Sunday at the town, and not lose two days by waiting. "No, it is our custom," was Manenko's reply, and all he could say was answered in the same "pertinacious lady style."

On Sunday afternoon messengers came from Shinte, who expressed his approbation of the objects had in view by the travelers in their

CHILDREN'S GAMES.

journey through the country, and his pleasure at the prospect that a way would be opened for the visits of white men, giving him opportunity to purchase ornaments of them at pleasure.

The next day, when Manenko thought the sun was high enough to make a lucky entrance, the party came into the town. They found it embowered in banana and other tropical trees of broad leaf. The streets present a remarkable contrast to those of the Bechuana towns in the fact that they are straight. Here Livingstone for the first time saw native huts with square walls and round roofs. Around the huts were courts or yards, inclosed with fences remarkably straight, which were made with upright poles neatly interwoven with grass or leafy bushes. In these courts were small plantations of tobacco, sugar-cane, bananas, and a little salinaceous plant used as a relish. The Balonda, among whom we now are traveling, are real negroes, having much more wool on their heads and bodies than any of the Caffre or Bechuana tribes. They are generally of very dark color, but occasionally one may be seen of lighter hue. The greater part of them have thick lips, flat noses, and heads elongated backward and upward.

On Tuesday, about eleven o'clock, Shinte honored his visitors with a grand reception. The

kotla, or place of audience, was about one hundred yards square. Near one side stood two graceful banian trees. Under one of these Shinte sat
upon a sort of throne which was covered with a
leopard's skin. He was dressed in a checked
jacket, and a kilt of scarlet baize edged with
green. On his head he wore a helmet made of
beads neatly woven together, and crowned with
a large bunch of goose-feathers. Armlets and
bracelets of iron and copper covered his limbs,
and many strings of large beads hung from his
neck. Close to him sat three lads with large
quivers of arrows resting on their shoulders.

When our friends entered the kotla the whole
of Manenko's party saluted Shinte by clapping
their hands, and Sambanza did obeisance by rubbing his arms and chest with ashes. Livingstone
and his party retired to one of the unoccupied
trees, for the sake of the shade. They were in
good position to witness the whole ceremony,
being about forty yards from the chief. The different sections of the tribe now came forward
and saluted the chief by clapping the hands, the
head man of each company making obeisance
with ashes, after the fashion just mentioned.
Then came the soldiers, with drawn swords, and
armed to the teeth, twisting their faces, to look
as savage as possible, and shouting, and running

toward the white man and his party, with the apparent purpose of testing their courage. Finding the strangers were not to be frightened in that way, they turned round, saluted Shinte, and retired.

When all were seated, the curious capering usually seen at pichos began. A man starts up and imitates the most approved movements and attitudes of an actual battle. He throws a javelin, receives another on his shield, springs to one side to avoid a third; he then leaps and runs backward and forward. This ceremony over, Sambanza and the spokesman of Nyamoána stalked back and forth in front of Shinte, relating in a loud voice all they had been able to learn of the white man and his people. They spoke of his connection with the Makololo, the return of the captives, the Bible as the Word of God, the desire to open the country for trade, the wish for the tribes to live in peace, adding he ought to have taught the Makololo that first, for the Balonda had never attacked them, yet they had assailed the Balonda; perhaps he is fibbing, perhaps not; but as Shinte had never done harm to any one, and the Balonda had good hearts, he had better receive the white man well and send him on his way.

Sambanza was very gayly attired, having a

cloth so long that a boy carried it as a train. He had, too, a profusion of beads.

Behind Shinte were seated about one hundred women dressed in red baize. The principal wife of Shinte sat in front, with a curious red cap on her head. During the pauses between the speeches these ladies chanted a sort of plaintive ditty, but whether it was applause of the speakers themselves, or Shinte, the visitors could not tell. A party of musicians went round the kotla several times. It consisted of three drummers and four performers on the piano, or "marimba." This instrument "consists of two bars of wood placed side by side, here quite straight, but further north bent round so as to resemble half the tire of a carriage wheel; across these are placed about fifteen wooden keys, each of which is two or three inches broad and fifteen or eighteen inches long." The thickness of the bars "is regulated according to the deepness of the note required. Each of the keys has a calabash beneath it; from the upper part of each a portion is cut off, to enable them to embrace the bars, and form hollow sounding-boards to the keys, which also are of different sizes, according to the note required, and little drumsticks elicit the music. Rapidity of execution seems much admired among them, and the music is pleasant to the ear. In Angola

the Portuguese use the marimba in their dances."
Their drums are beaten with the hands. They
are neatly carved from the trunk of a tree. A
small hole in the side is covered by a bit of a
spider's web. The head is made of antelope
skin. It is tightened by holding it to the fire
till the heat contracts it.

Nine speakers made orations. Then Shinte
and all the people stood up. The chief had
maintained true African dignity during the whole
ceremony. Livingstone's men noticed, however,
that Shinte had kept his eyes on the white man
all the while. About one thousand persons were
present at this "picho," or public meeting for the
reception of the white missionary.

The following night Livingstone was awakened, at an unseasonable hour, by a message
from Shinte requesting a visit. Kolimbota, his
guide, thought he ought to go, but he, being
sick with fever, refused to do so, insisting· that
he ought to have some choice in the matter.
He "was neither a hyena nor a witch, and hated
words of the night and deeds of darkness." This
highly offended the guide.

At ten next morning they went, and were
conducted into the courts of Shinte. The walls
of the inclosure were of woven poles, very neat
and high. Within it many trees were planted.

affording a grateful shade. They sat beneath a Ficus India tree, which showed its relationship to the banian of India by sending down shoots toward the ground. The chief soon came, having the appearance of a man about fifty-five years of age, of medium hight, with a frank, open countenance. He seemed in good temper, and said he had expected on the day before, at the reception, "that a man who came from the gods would have approached and talked to him." And this had been Livingstone's intention; but the sight of Shinte's own men keeping at such a distance from him, and the formidable preparations led him to yield to the solicitations of his party, and remain by the tree where they first seated themselves. This remark, however, confirmed the missionary in his previous opinion that with these Africans a frank and fearless bearing is the most winning. During this interview Livingstone stated the object of his journey, and the chief expressed his approval by clapping his hands. He then replied through a spokesman, and all present responded by clapping hands.

When the more important business was dispatched, Livingstone asked the old chief if he had ever seen a white man before, when he replied, "Never; you are the very first I have ever seen with a white skin and straight hair; your clothing, too, is different from any we have ever seen." On learning from some of his people that "Shinte's mouth was bitter for want of tasting ox-flesh," Livingstone made him a present of an ox, with which he was greatly delighted. He advised the chief to open a trade in cows with the Makololo. This advice he afterward adopted.

When Manenko heard of the gift of an ox to her uncle, she came to our friend the missionary and insisted that she had been slighted and wronged; that "this white man belonged to her; she had brought him here, and therefore the ox was hers, not Shinte's." She then ordered her men to slaughter it, and presented Shinte with a leg only, and he did not resent her action in the matter.

Next morning Livingstone was awakened early with a message from the chief inviting him to another interview, but the raging thirst of a high fever having been just alleviated by sudden perspiration, he declined the honor for a few hours. When he did go Shinte could not be found— most likely because the divination was unfavorable. When he had returned to bed another messenger came to inform him that "Shinte wished to say all he had to tell him at once." The offer was too tempting to decline. The chief met him

with a present of a fowl, a basket of manioc
meal, and a calabash of mead. He said these
attacks of fever were the only thing which would
hinder the success of the journey, for he had
men who would guide the white man, and who
knew all the paths to the sea. He himself had
traveled when young. When asked what he
would recommend for the fever, he said, "Drink
plenty of the mead, and as it gets in it will drive
the fever out." He seemed to like the remedy
very much when he had no fever. It was pretty
strong.

Shinte had always been a friend to Sebituane,
and now that his son Sekeletu was in his place
he was more than a friend—a father—to him.
He was highly pleased with the large calabashes
of clarified butter which Sekeletu had sent him,
and wished to retain Kolimbota, that he might
send back a present to Sekeletu by his hands.
Livingstone afterward discovered that this prop-
osition originated with Kolimbota himself. He
wished to escape the danger to which he might
be exposed by the ferocity of the tribes through
which they were to pass, of which he now heard
a great deal.

The Balonda of this village were remarkably
punctilious in their manners. Whenever they
meet their superiors on the street they drop

upon their knees and rub dust on their arms and chest. Sambanza kneeled in this way while the son of Shinte was passing him. The woman who draws water for the chief rings a bell to warn all persons to keep out of her way, lest they might exert an evil influence upon the drink of the great chief. It would be a very grave offense to come near her when bearing water for her lord. The effect of the slave-trade in this part of the country upon the public conscience is seen in the custom which prevails of selling the poor or their children to the Mambari, or half-breed Portuguese traders. An instance illustrating the custom occurred during Livingstone's visit. A young man of Lobale fled into the country of Shinte, and located himself without first reporting to the chief. For this offense he was seized and offered for sale. No chief in the south would have treated him in this way. All of the attendants of our traveler were horrified at the act, and the Makololo and Barotse both declared that if the Balonda knew how their chiefs treated fugitives there would be very few of the discontented remaining with Shinte.

Another incident of a similar kind, totally unlike any thing which occurs among the southern tribes, may be mentioned. Two children, of seven years, living about a quarter of a mile from the village,

went out from their home but a short distance
to gather a little firewood, and were kidnapped.
The afflicted parents could find no trace of them.
There were no beasts of prey, and it took place
so near the town that our missionary suspected
it was the work of some of the men high in rank
at Shinte's court. In such cases the parents
have no redress. Even Shinte himself seems to
have been engaged in this same infamous trade.
One night he sent for Livingstone and presented
him with a slave girl about ten years old, saying
he was always in the habit of presenting his visitors with a child. The missionary thanked him
for his expression of kindness, but told him he
thought it wrong to take away children from
their parents, and desired him to give up this
system altogether, and trade in ivory, beeswax,
and cattle. He urged that she was "to be a
child" to bring him water, and that a great man
ought to have a child for such a purpose. When
Livingstone replied that he had four children,
and should feel very sorry if his chief should
take his little girl from him and give her away,
and that he preferred the little girl should remain and bring water for her mother, he sent for
one a head taller, thinking he was dissatisfied
with the first. This was likewise declined, with
many explanations of the evil of slavery.

An amusing and interesting scene was witnessed when Livingstone exhibited his magic lantern in the presence of Shinte, his principal men, and the same crowd of court ladies who graced the grand reception with their presence. The chief was very anxious to see the pictures, but on account of his own illness our traveler was obliged to put him off for several days. When at last he was able to gratify this eager desire, the first picture shown was that of Abraham offering up his son Isaac. The picture was shown as large as life. The knife was uplifted, and just in the act of striking the lad. The Balonda men said the picture was more like a god than the things of clay and wood which they worshiped. Livingstone explained to them that this man was the first of a race to whom God had given the Bible. The women listened in silence and awe. But when the slide was moved the upraised dagger moved toward them. They thought it was to be buried in their bodies instead of Isaac's, and they all shouted at once, "Mother, mother," and ran away pellmell, tumbling over tobacco bushes, idol huts, and each other in their fright. Shinte sat bravely through the whole exhibition, and then examined the instrument with great interest; but the ladies could not be coaxed back again.

Careful explanations were given, so that no one should think there was any thing supernatural about it. "It was the only mode of instruction," says our missionary, "I was ever pressed to repeat. The people came long distances for the express purpose of seeing the objects and hearing the explanations."

Heavy showers were now falling every day, and the long-used tent had become rotten and leaky. Surgical instruments were rusted, clothing mildewed, shoes moldy, and bedding wet. The sunshine only lasted a short time in the afternoon. Thus was our traveler delayed in his preparations for a start on his continued journey.

CHAPTER VII.

A PRINCELY GIFT—MANIOC—SUPERSTITION OF THE NA-
TIVES—KATEMA—BIRDS—SPIDERS—ANTS—SWIMMING A
RIVER—PROSPECT OF A FIGHT.

ON the morning when Livingstone expected
to renew his journey Sambanza was sent
off early for the guides. But he returned about
midday, drunk, and without them. "This was
the first case of real babbling intoxication we
had seen in this region. The boyaloa, or beer
of the country has more of a stupefying than
exciting nature; hence the beer-bibbers are great
sleepers; they may frequently be seen lying on
their faces, sound asleep. This peculiarity of
posture was ascribed by no less an authority
than Aristotle to wine, while those who were
sent asleep by beer were believed 'to lie on their
backs.'" The mead such as Shinte had presented his guest the other day is much stronger
than boyaloa. It was excessive drinking of this
that intoxicated Sambanza.

Just before his departure Shinte came to the
white man's tent for a last interview. He looked

with very great interest at the looking-glass, books, quicksilver, hair-brushes, comb, watch, and other curiosities. He pointed out the principal guide, whom he said he had ordered to remain with the missionary till he reached the sea. But this language was figurative somewhat. After reaching the next chief, Katema, the guides were to return, but the good words they would speak in Livingstone's behalf to that chief would help him on to the sea. The white man had now left Sekeletu far behind, he said, and must now look to Shinte alone for aid. During this interview Shinte closed the tent, that none of his people might witness his extravagance, and then drew out from his clothing a string of beads and the end of a conical shell which is valued very highly among the natives as evidence of distinction. He hung it around the neck of his guest, saying, "There, now you *have* a proof of my friendship." These shells are prized so highly that a slave may be bought for two of them, and five would be regarded as a handsome price for an elephant's tusk worth fifty dollars.

Eight of Shinte's men accompanied our party of travelers to aid in carrying the luggage. They passed in a northerly direction down the lovely valley in which the town stands. Then bearing to the west, they passed through a beautiful open forest, and spent the night at a Balonda village. The country through which they passed was much like that before described on this journey—flat, with open forests. During the first day's travel a fine range of green hills was seen off to the right, abounding in iron ore, which is worked by Shinte's people.

In every valley villages of from twenty to thirty huts were found, surrounded by gardens of manioc or cassava. This root is the staff of life in this region of country. It is very easily cultivated. The earth is thrown up in oblong beds about three feet in width. In these beds pieces of manioc stalk are planted four feet apart. Beans or ground nuts are sown between them. When these are harvested the ground is cleared of weeds. In from ten to eighteen months the manioc roots are fit for food. But there is no necessity that they be gathered immediately, as they are good and edible for three years. Then they become bitter and dry. Every part of the plant is useful. The leaves may be cooked like a vegetable. The stalk grows to a hight of six feet. When a woman digs up the roots she plants a piece or two of the upper stalk in the hole she has made, and a new crop begins.

The roots are twelve to eighteen inches long, and three or four in diameter. There are two varieties, one sweet and wholesome, the other bitter and containing poison. This last-named variety is of much more rapid growth, which secures its perpetuation. The natives extract the poison by placing it four days in a pool of water. It then becomes partially decomposed. It is now taken out of the water, the skin stripped off, and the root exposed to the sun. When dried it is easily pounded into a fine white meal which resembles starch very closely, both in flavor and appearance. Often, however, it has a little of the peculiar taste caused by partial decomposition. When used as food the manioc meal is stirred into boiling water, one man stirring the porridge, while another holds the kettle. Livingstone represents it as being just about as palatable as starch made from diseased potatoes. But this is the common food of the country, and he was obliged by hunger to eat it. He could barely manage to swallow it sweetened with a little honey.

Intemese, the chief guide furnished by Shinte, sent messages to the villages along the route that the friends of their chief must have abundance of provisions. To these orders the people responded with liberality, presenting Livingstone and his attendants with far more food than was furnished by Shinte himself.

It was soon observed that these new guides were far more careful and particular in their notions of etiquette than the tribes farther south. They gave food to Livingstone and his Makololo attendants, . but would not take it from them when they had cooked it. Nor would they eat in the presence of these their superiors. The Makololo, accustomed at home to the most free and easy manners, frequently offered handfuls of food to any of the Balonda who happened to be near. But they would not taste it. They are very punctilious in their manners toward each other. Each hut has its own fire. And when it goes out, they will not take from a neighbor, but kindle it afresh for themselves. Many of these customs, doubtless, arise from superstitious fear.

Away from the villages, in the deep, dark forests, instead of the idols representing the head of a lion, or man, or the crooked stick smeared with medicines, there are outlines of human faces cut in the bark of the trees, closely resembling those seen on Egyptian monuments. Offerings of manioc roots, or ears of corn, are placed on branches. Every few miles you find heaps of sticks, on which each one passing throws a branch, after the fashion of cairns, in ancient Britain. Sometimes a few sticks are placed on the path, and each traveler turns aside, and a sudden bend is made in the road. The minds of these people seem filled with fear and dread of superior beings, whom they fancy reside in these gloomy forests. And hence, these offerings are made to propitiate them.

The dress of the Balonda men is made of the skins of the smaller game, such as the jackal, or wild cat. They are dressed so as to be soft and pliable, and hung from a girdle around the loins. "The dress of the women is of a nondescript character; but they were not immodest."

On the 7th of February the travelers reached the village of Soano Molopo, a half-brother of the chief Katema. When visited, he was found sitting with about one hundred men around him. Although private information had, undoubtedly, been given him, he called upon Intemese for some account of the white man and his companions. And in reply to the statements of the guide he said, "The journey of the white man is very proper; but Shinte has disturbed us by showing the path to the Makololo who accompany him. He ought to have taken them through the country without showing them the towns. We are afraid of the Makololo." He then gave his visitors a handsome present of food. Intemese, by telling this chief what Livingstone had given to Shinte and others, by importunities and threats, tried to force the gift of an ox to Soano Molopo. And when the company were ready to move onward the guide refused to start. So they packed up and went on without him, leaving him to overtake them at his leisure. His principal value to them was in introducing them to the villagers as they passed along; preventing any alarm on account of their visit, and speaking a good word for them, which had considerable influence with the natives.

Heavy rains were falling, and they were glad to make booths for shelter at the house of Mozinkwa. He was a most intelligent and friendly man, belonging to the chief Katema. His children were very black, but comely. They were all by one mother. And Livingstone says they "were the finest negro family I ever saw." He had a fine, large garden in cultivation. The fence around his courtyard was made of the banian, which, taking root, had grown to a live hedge. His wife had cotton growing around her premises, with the castor-oil plant, relishes of various kinds, and a larger shrub which yields a purgative oil. The generous, frank friendship, and liberal hospitality of this man and his wife would have won admiration if shown by the most civilized people. Mozinkwa's wife asked Livingstone to bring her a cloth from the white man's country. But when he came that way again she was in her grave. These natives can not bear to live on a spot where a favorite wife has died. They only visit it afterward, to pray to her, or make some offering. In accordance with this custom, Mozinkwa had abandoned his garden, trees, and huts to ruin.

After leaving this hospitable mansion, while crossing a river, the travelers were met by a messenger from Katema, named Shakatwala. He was a sort of steward, such as these native chiefs each have attached to their person. They are generally poor, but men of shrewdness and ability. He informed our travelers that Katema had received no definite information respecting him, but if his objects were peaceful he was invited to come to the town of the chief, as Katema loved strangers.

Crossing the river Sotembwa, they came to the town, about eight miles beyond. It was a group of villages rather than a town. They were conducted about a half mile from the houses, to prepare lodgings for themselves; while Intemese, the guide, was taken to the chief, to undergo examination as to the character and objects of the white man and his companions. Katema soon sent them a present of food. Next morning a formal presentation to the chief was granted. Katema was seated on a sort of throne, with about three hundred men sitting on the ground around him, and thirty women — his wives—close behind him. The main body of the people were seated in a semicircle, about fifty yards distant. The head man of each party stood a little in front, ready to come near the chief at his call, for council. Intemese now gave an account of the white man. Katema then presented sixteen large baskets of meal, half a dozen fowls, and a dozen eggs, expressing his regret that the strangers had slept hungry. "Go home," said he, "cook and eat; and then you will be in a fit state to speak to me at an audience I will give you to-morrow."

This chief is a tall man, about forty years old. He was dressed in a snuff-brown coat, with a broad band of tinsel running down the arms. On his head was a helmet of beads and feathers. He held in his hand a large tail, made of the caudal extremities of several gnus. This wand has charms attached, to defend his person from evil influences. He waved it constantly. He seemed in good spirits—indulging frequently in a hearty laugh. This Livingstone thought a good sign ; as a mirthful man is seldom hard to deal with.

At his visit next morning, Katema addressed

the traveler with these words, "I am the great Moene or lord Katema, the fellow of Matiamvo. There is no one in the country equal to Matiamvo and me. I have always lived here, and my forefathers too. There is the house in which my father lived. You found no human skulls near the place where you encamped. I never killed any of the traders. They all come to me. I am the great Moene Katema of whom you have heard." Livingstone thought he looked as though he had fallen asleep when tipsy, and had been dreaming of his greatness. On making known his objects, the chief immediately offered him three guides, who he said would conduct the white man by a new route, avoiding the water-covered plains on the ordinary path of the traders. "This was more suited to our wishes, for we never found a path safe that had been trodden by slave-traders." Livingstone, in these words, is not very complimentary to the traders, but quite as much so as they deserve.

Katema had a herd of about thirty splendid cattle. Livingstone complimented him on their possession, and told him how he might milk the cows. The cattle are mostly white, and quite wild, running off at the approach of a stranger, with the graceful ease of a herd of elands. The Makololo admired them very much. It seemed strange that all the people did not possess cattle, in a country which furnished such luxuriant pasturage.

Katema made no offer of an ox, as a Makololo, or Caffre chief would have done. So our party were obliged to slaughter one of their own. After living so long on the light Balonda porridge and green corn, a supply of beef was highly relished.

Birds of song are abundant here, especially near the villages—making the mornings cheerful with their merry chorus. Canaries are numerous, with the back colored a yellowish-green, a darker longitudinal band meeting in the center, and a narrow, dark band passing from the bill over the eye, and back to the bill again. A pretty little songster, a species of canary, called "cabazo," is kept in cages by the natives. When asked why they kept them in confinement, they replied, " Because they sing sweetly." The cages are very neatly made, having traps on the top to catch other birds. It seems remarkable there should be such numbers of feathered songsters in a country where there is such a scarcity of game and all animal life. There are none of the larger kinds of fowls. The rivers contain very few fish. Common flies are less plenty than in other parts of the country, and musketoes are

rarely numerous enough to disturb the sleep of a
weary man.

But the country is not free from all insect
plagues. When just falling asleep one night,
Livingstone felt something running across his
forehead, and putting up his hand to brush it
away, was sharply stung both on the hand and
the head. When a light was brought, it was
found the mischief had been wrought by a light-
colored spider, about half an inch in length. The
pain occasioned by the bite ceased in about two
hours, without any remedy. The Bechuanas
believe there is a black spider in the country
whose bite is fatal. No instance of death from
this cause was known to Livingstone during his
whole stay in the country. There is, however, a
large, hairy, black spider frequently seen, an inch
and a quarter long, and three-fourths of an inch
broad; having a process at the end of its front
claws, similar to that at the end of a scorpion's
tail; and when the bulbous part of it is pressed,
the poison oozes out at the point. There are
several varieties of spiders in the south, which
seize their prey by leaping upon it from a distance of several inches. When frightened they
can leap a foot.

A large, reddish spider hunts its prey in a
style peculiar to itself. It does not lie in ambush

or catch its game at a single bound. It runs
about with very great rapidity, dodging in and
out, behind and around every object, seeking
what it may devour. Its great size and rapid
movements make it frightful to any one not well
acquainted with its habits. Yet it does no harm.
The natives call it selali. It is believed to be
the maker of an ingenious hinged cover for its
nest. You see a door about the size of an English shilling, and on the inside, which is lying
upward, it is made of a white, silky substance,
like paper. It lies beside a deep hole. Attempting to lift it, you find it fastened by a hinge on
one side. When you turn it over the hole, it
fits exactly, and the outer side is coated over
with earth, just like that around the mouth of
the nest; so that when the door is closed it is
impossible to detect it. Hence the nest is never
seen except when its owner is out—having left
the door open.

Another variety of spider is a large, beautiful,
yellow-spotted insect, which makes a web a yard
in diameter. The lines on which the web is sus-
pended are about the size of coarse thread, and
extend from one tree to another. Still another
kind of these busy insects makes its webs so
numerous and thick as often to hide the trunk
of a tree from sight, or cover a piece of hedge

so completely with them that its branches can
not be seen.

The ants in this country maintain the reputation of their species, for wisdom. They live on
these low water-covered plains, where the whole
country is submerged so large a portion of the
year that the lotus, and other water plants, ma-
ture. They maintain their existence by building
little houses of black, tough loam, on stalks of
grass, above the line of inundation. These upper chambers must, of course, be built during
the dry season, for only then could they obtain
the material for building. Who taught the ants
this wisdom and foresight, so that they anticipate
the coming flood?

But let us return to our journeying. Crossing
the watery plains to the dry lands beyond, our
company found themselves on the watershed, between the northern and southern rivers. The
villages here own the authority of the chief Ka-
tende. At the first village the travelers were
treated very kindly, and the guides Katema had
furnished turned back.

Passing on from this village our company
passed through a beautiful valley, thickly covered with tall trees. Many of them presented
sixty or eighty feet of straight trunk before the
first branch appeared. Graceful flowers bloomed

beneath their shade. A stream ran through the valley, which was crossed by a rustic bridge; now submerged thigh-deep. Three days of travel now brought them to the Kasai or Lake—a beautiful river, resembling the Clyde in Scotland, and about one hundred yards wide. It flows alternately through beautiful bowers of silvan vegetation and rich meadows, covered with tall grass. Kangenke, the head man of a village in this locality, furnished guides, and canoes, to cross the river. The men pointed out its course, and said, "Though you sail for months, you will turn without seeing the end of it."

A trick was here played upon one of Livingstone's men, which may help illustrate the character of the people, among whom he was now traveling. A knife was purposely dropped near the encampment, the owner watching till it was picked up by one of the men. Nothing was said till the party were divided in crossing the river; one-half on this side and the rest on the other bank. Then the charge was made to Livingstone, that one of his men had stolen a knife. Confident of the honesty of his attendants, he asked the man making the charge to search the baggage. The unfortunate lad who had picked up the knife then came forward and confessed he had it in a basket which had been carried

across the river. When it was returned, the
owner refused to receive it unless it was accompanied by a fine. This was his plan in the whole
affair, to extort gifts in this wav. The lad offered
beads. But they were refused with contempt;
and a costly ornament of shell, such as we have
before mentioned as Shinte's present, was demanded. And the lad was obliged to part with
that. There was no other escape from the im-
position. The young man ought to have brought
any article found, to Livingstone, as this was the
custom of the whole party. Shinte's people had
forewarned them of such like dishonorable tricks
practiced by these people.

The villagers here made no presents of food,
and charged exorbitant prices for the little meal
and manioc they brought for sale. They, however, know nothing of the value of money. Gold
is unknown, and trade is carried on in the form
of barter. Gunpowder was in great demand. A
good-sized fowl was sold for a single charge.
Unfortunately our travelers had too meager a
supply to take advantage of this feature of the
market here. Next to gunpowder, English calico
and beads were sought after by the natives.

When they had traveled some distance away
from the villages, the guides Kangenke had given
them sat down, and refused to go farther with-

out the present of a cloth. They said there were three paths in front, and they would leave the white man to take whichever he pleased, unless their demand was complied with. Livingstone knew the direction in which he was to go, and desired his men to go on without them. But Mashauana feared they might wander, and asked permission to give his own cloth. When this was brought out to view, the guides came forward, shouting "Averie! Averie!" This exclamation seems to be of Christian origin—a corruption of Ave Marie. Elsewhere among these people an exclamation of surprise, " Allah," was noticed, which sounds like the Illah of the Arabs.

They came, in the afternoon of February 29th, to a tributary of the Lake. The bridge was covered with water up to the breasts of the men. And at each end they were obliged to swim. Some of them held on to the tail of an ox while crossing. Livingstone intended to adopt this method, but when he reached the deep water, and dismounted, the ox dashed off to join his companions before the helm could be caught. He sank so deep in the water that Livingstone failed in the attempt to catch hold of the blanket belt; and when he pulled the bridle, the ox seemed likely to come backward on him. So he

struck out for the opposite bank alone. His
men were terribly frightened when they saw him
parted from the ox; not knowing he could swim.
About twenty of them rushed simultaneously into
the water, for his rescue. And just as he reached
the bank, one seized his arm, and another threw
his arm around the body of the white man.
Some leaped off the bridge, and their cloaks
floated down the stream. Part of his goods,
abandoned in the excitement of the moment,
were brought up from the bottom, after he was
safe. Though he did not need their aid, Livingstone felt very grateful for the earnest and generous efforts they made for his rescue, when they
thought his life in peril. They were highly
pleased to find he could swim, like themselves,
without the aid of an ox tail. Afterward some
villagers tried to frighten them, by telling of the
deep rivers that were in their way. The men
laughed at them and said, "We can all swim;
who carried the white man across the river but
himself?" He says he felt proud of their praise.

  This fidelity and generous devotion shown by
these uncivilized men to a stranger, and one of
another race, speaks well, most certainly, for
their native virtue and goodness of heart.

  Livingstone's Makololo companions were frequently heard lamenting, as they passed through

NJAMBI AT HOME

these lovely and fertile valleys, that they were
left uncultivated. "What a fine country for cattle!" they often said; "My heart is sore to see
such fruitful valleys for corn lying waste." Livingstone at first thought the reason why the people in this splendid country kept no cattle, was
because the despotism of their chiefs would take
them from the common people. But he afterward came to the conclusion that the country
had been infested by tsetse, so that cattle could
not be kept. And now that the Balonda had
come into possession of fire-arms, they had killed
off all the large game on which the insect feeds,
and thus starved it out. This pest gone, cattle
would now do finely here, as the success of a few
chiefs we have named fully shows.

The village of Njambi, one of the chiefs of the
Chiboque, was reached on the 4th of March.
Intending to pass the Sabbath here, and the provisions being exhausted, Livingstone ordered a
riding ox to be slaughtered. The hump and ribs
were sent to Njambi, with the statement that
this was the usual tribute to chiefs, in the part
of the country the travelers had come from. He
in return expressed his thanks, and promised to
send food. But next morning he sent a very
small present of meal, and an impudent message,
demanding a man, an ox, a gun, powder, cloth, or

a shell; and intimated his purpose, in case of refusal, to prevent the further progress of the travelers.

About midday Njambi came with all his men and surrounded Livingstone's encampment. His young men drew their swords, and brandished them very fiercely. And some of them pointed their guns at Livingstone, at the same time nodding at their comrades. The attendants of the missionary seized their javelins, and stood on the defensive. He sat on a çamp-stool, with his double-barreled gun across his knees. The chief, being invited to sit down, took a seat with his counselors, on the ground, near Livingstone. His men armed with spears quietly surrounded them. He now asked the chief what crime they had committed, that he had come out against them armed in that manner. The chief replied that one of the men of the white man's party, Pitsane, had, while sitting by the fire that morning, in spitting, allowed a little saliva to fall on the leg of one of his men; and for that "guilt" he demanded a fine of an ox, a man, or a gun. Pitsane admitted the fact, but explained it as purely an accident, and said he wiped off the saliva with his hand soon as it fell. In reply to the demand for a fine, Livingstone said they would all die before they would give up one of

their number as a slave. They were all free
men. "Then you can give the gun with which
the ox was shot," said the Chiboque. This prop-
osition was declined, on the ground that it would
be giving them additional power to plunder the
white man and his party—which they evidently
wanted to do.

This they denied, and said they only wanted
the customary tribute, for passing through the
country. Livingstone told them if he trod on
their gardens he would pay them; but not for
walking on the ground of God, our common
Father. Now they turned attention to the crime
of the spitting. And the chief insisting, when
questioned, that he really thought it a matter of
guilt, Livingstone gave him a shirt.

But the young Chiboque were dissatisfied.
And shouting and brandishing their swords,
they demanded a larger fine. At the request of
Pitsane, that something more be given, a bunch
of beads was offered. The counselors com-
plained, and a handkerchief was added. More
and more unreasonable grew the demands, ás
they were yielded to; the weapons being brandished furiously meanwhile. One young man made
a charge at Livingstone's head from behind, but
he swinging round the muzzle of his gun to
the mouth of his assailant, he quickly retreated.

The missionary then told the chief and his counselors, that as *they* refused to be satisfied with any thing that could be offered, it was plain *they* wanted to fight; while he only wanted to pass peaceably through the country. They must begin first, and bear the guilt before God. He and his party would not strike the first blow.

He knew very well that the Chiboque would aim first at the white man. But he had four gun barrels ready for instant action. So he took care to appear perfectly calm; and looked quietly around upon the savage scene. The chief and his counselors being in greater danger than Livingstone, and seeing the cool preparation of his men, thought it prudent not to accept his challenge and strike the first blow.

At last they said, "You come among us in a new way, and say you are quite friendly: how can we know it, unless you give us some of your food, and take some of ours? If you give us an ox, we will give you whatever you wish, and we will be friends." This proposal was accepted, and an ox was given. Njambi asked what the strangers wished, and was told they were most in need of food. In the evening he sent them a very small basket of meal, and two or three pounds of the meat of their own ox! with the apology that he had no fowls, and very little food of any kind. Our traveler was much gratified with the coolness and bravery exhibited by his men on this occasion. But though he felt sure of being able with his Makololo, who had been drilled by Sebituane, to beat back double the number of his assailants, he was exceedingly glad to avoid the shedding of blood.

Passing onward through a succession of open lawns, and deep forests, it was interesting to notice the instinct of the trees. One was noticed especially, which, when cut, emits a milky juice. When growing on the open lawns, it is an ordinary umbrageous tree, having no disposition to be a climber. But when growing in the forest it takes the same form, and then sends out a climbing branch, which twines around another tree, rising in that way thirty or forty feet, till on a level with the tops of the surrounding tree. There it spreads out a second crown, where it can enjoy a fair share of sunlight. In more dense portions of the forest it takes the form of a climber, only making no attempt at forming a lower head.

The paths through some of these forests were very narrow, and incumbered with gigantic creepers. The peculiar traits of character which distinguished Livingstone's riding ox, "Sinbad," were here pretty fully developed. His back was softer than the others, but his temper was more intractable. His horns bent downward, and hung loosely, so he could do no harm with them. But every now and then he would suddenly dart aside from the narrow path. The bridle consists of a string tied to a stick, which is put through the cartilage of the nose. If you jerk this, " Sinbad," instead of stopping, as a well-disposed ox ought, only runs on the faster. Nothing will stop him but a stroke of the wand across the nose. When you attempt to turn him aside, he allows his head and nose to follow the bridle, but keeps his eye on the forbidden spot, and goes in spite of you. Now and then he would run under a climber or vine stretched across the path so low that his rider could not stoop under it, and when he was thus dragged to the ground, " Sinbad" never missed the opportunity without attempting to express his affection for his master by a kick.

•Livingstone suffered a good deal with fever, and sometimes the party were delayed a day or two at a time by his illness. On one occasion some of his men made a sort of mutiny, because they thought him partial in the distribution of some gifts of beads. He explained that the beads given to his principal men were for the purchase of meal. On Sunday following, while lying sick in his tent; he was greatly disturbed by the terrible noise made by some of these mutineers, in preparing a skin they had procured. He sent his attendant twice with the request that they would be quiet, as the noise pained him. But they paid no attention to the request; and when he had put out his head and repeated it, he was answered by an impudent laugh. Knowing that every thing depended on the maintenance of discipline, he seized a double-barreled pistol, and rushing out, put them all to a precipitate flight. To those who remained within hearing, he said that they must remember he was master, and must maintain discipline even at the expense of some of their limbs. They were all satisfied of his determination, and never afterward gave him any trouble. Reaching the banks of the Quango on the 4th of April, the natives, called Bashinje, were asked to lend canoes for the company to cross the river. This brought out the chief, who said all the canoe men were his children, and could do nothing without his authority. He then made the usual demand for a man, an ox, or a gun. Otherwise, he said, the strangers must return to the country from which they had come. This chief was a young man. His woolly hair was very elaborately dressed; on the back of his head it was put up in the form of a cone, about eight inches in diameter at the base, and carefully swathed with red and black thread. The only thing Livingstone had to give in response to his demand, was a blanket. And he feared if the Bashinje chief got possession of this before the party were ferried over, they would still be detained to extort further tribute from them. So he tried to persuade his men to go forward and get possession of the canoes. But they feared the chief would attack them while crossing. They stripped off the last of their copper rings and gave him, but this did not satisfy him. Just at this juncture a young half-caste Portuguese sergeant made his appearance, and urged the party to go forward in spite of the Bashinje. He had come across the Quango in search of bees-wax.

As they moved away from the chief, his people opened fire upon them, and continued it for some time. But they escaped unharmed, and moving quietly forward, without running, as their assailants had thought they would do, they were not pursued any considerable distance. Cypriano, the militia sergeant, assisted in making an arrangement with the ferrymen more advantageous than the gift of the blanket. Once across to the opposite bank, and they were in the territory of the Bangala, who are subject to the

Portuguese. Then all their troubles with the border tribes were at an end.

Three miles west of the river they came to a collection of neat, square houses, with many cleanly, half-caste Portuguese standing in front of them. The men are all enrolled in the militia, and Cypriano is the commander of the division established here. No pay is given to them by the government. They engage in trade and agriculture for a livelihood, and live among the Bangala, who are their vassals.

The company reached the house of Cypriano after dark, and Livingstone pitched his tent in front of it. In the morning, after giving his men a generous supply of corn and pumpkins, Cypriano invited Livingstone to breakfast. The meal consisted of ground nuts and roasted corn, then boiled manioc roots, with guavas and honey for dessert. To the tired and hungry traveler it was a magnificent breakfast, for which he felt very grateful. At dinner the sergeant was equally bountiful. And some of his friends came in to aid our friend, the missionary, in doing justice to the hospitality of his kind and generous host. Before eating the hands were washed in water poured upon them by a female slave. One of the guests cut up a fowl with a knife and fork. But neither forks nor spoons were used in eating.

The repast was eaten with decency and good manners, and concluded by washing hands as at the beginning. The hospitality of Cypriano culminated in slaughtering an ox for his guests. All of these Portuguese could read and write easily. They possessed a few books—a small work on medicine, a Portuguese dictionary, and a small cyclopedia. The dictionary gave a definition of the word priest, which savors very strongly of Catholic notions; namely, "one who takes care of the conscience." Neither Cypriano nor his companions knew any thing about the Bible. But they had relics in german-silver cases, hung upon their necks, to act as charms and protect them from danger. What a pity that the Church to which they belong does not give them the Word of God in their own language!

CHAPTER VIII.

A FEW days' journey from the dwelling of his hospitable friend Cypriano brought Livingstone to Cassange, the farthest inland station of the Portuguese in Western Africa. He crossed several fine streams which empty into the Quango, and made most of the journey through grass which towered two feet above his head, and sometimes hung over the path, making one side wet with dew in the morning, and when it rained, kept him wet all day. His clothing was so badly worn that he made his appearance among the people of the town in rather a forlorn condition. The first gentleman he met asked if he had a passport, and said it was necessary to take him before the authorities. Livingstone, according to his own statement, was in a similar state of mind to that of persons who commit a petty crime in order to obtain the food and shelter of a prison. So he gladly accompanied the gentleman to the house of the commandant or Chefe, Senhor de

Silva Rego. Having shown his passport, Livingstone was invited to supper by the commandant. Being very hungry, he thought he must have seemed specially ravenous to the other gentlemen around the table. But they had traveled extensively, and seemed to appreciate his condition.

Captain Antonio Rodrigues Neves kindly invited him to make his home at his house. Next morning his generous host arrayed him in a suit of decent clothing. And during the whole time of his stay he was treated as kindly as a brother could have been. This kindness was extended to the whole party, who were furnished with a liberal supply of food free of charge.

The village is composed of thirty or forty traders' houses, scattered irregularly over an elevated spot, in the great Quango, or Cassange valley. The houses are surrounded by plantations of manioc and corn, with kitchen gardens in the rear, in which the common European vegetables are cultivated; such as potatoes, peas, cabbages, onions, tomatoes, etc. Guavas and bananas, from the size and abundance of the trees, would seem to have been introduced long ago, when the land was held by the natives. But orange, fig, pine-apple, and cashew trees have been more recently introduced. There are about forty Portuguese traders in the district, all of whom are officers in the militia. Many of them have become rich by sending out Pombeiros, or native traders, to the more remote parts of the country.

Livingstone was an object of great curiosity to these Portuguese. They thought him an agent of the British Government engaged in some new movement for the suppression of slavery. They could not imagine what a "missionario" wanted with latitudes and longitudes, which he was so carefully taking. Becoming better acquainted, they put amusing questions, such as, "Is it common for missionaries to be doctors?" "Are you a doctor of medicine and a doctor mathematico, too? You must be more than a missionary, to know how to calculate longitude." "Come, tell us what rank you hold in the English Army."

On the 16th of April the anniversary of the resurrection of Christ was celebrated as a day of rejoicing, though the Portuguese have no priests here. The colored population dressed up a figure representing Judas Iscariot, and, mounting him on an ox, paraded about the village. The slaves and free colored population dressed in their finest clothing, visited the principal merchants, wishing them "a good feast," and expected a present from each of them in. return. It was sometimes

refused, though frequently granted in the shape
of calico for new dresses. At ten, A. M., Livingstone went to the residence of the commandant. At a given signal two of the brass government guns commenced firing, to the great delight
of Livingstone's men, who have very exalted ideas
of the power of a cannon. The Portuguese flag
was hoisted, and trumpets sounded, as an expression of joy over the great event celebrated. All
the principal inhabitants of the village were invited to a feast at the house of Captain Neves.
At the dinner there were biscuits from America,
butter from Cork, beer from England, wine from
Portugal, and all manner of preserved foreign
fruits. No expense was spared to make the en-
tertainment rich and joyous. When the feasting
was over the company sat down to the common
amusement of card-playing — continuing it till
eleven o'clock at night.

These Portuguese gentlemen have no wives of
their own nation here. They come here to stay
a few years, make a little money, and return to
their native land. Hence they do not bring their
wives with them. But it is common for them to
have families by native women. The common
prejudice against color does not exist here. The
half-colored children are treated as well as though
they were pure white. Colored clerks sit at the

table with the merchants who employ them, without any embarrassment.

The tusks, sent by Sekeletu, were sold to the traders at Cassange. -Two muskets, three small barrels of gunpowder, and English calico, and baize enough to clothe the whole party of Livingstone's attendants, with large bunches of beads, were given for one tusk. This was highly satisfactory to the Makololo. They now began to abuse the traders who had visited them in their own country, and *cheated* them, as they said. Livingstone, however, tried to explain to them that these traders, if they carried their goods so far inland, could not sell at the same prices as they did here, on account of the great expense of traveling so far. When they went on to Loanda, and saw goods sold still more cheaply, they came to the conclusion it would be better for them to come to that city than to trade at Cassange.

Our traveler had now about three hundred miles to make in order to reach the coast. His men told him they had been thinking of turning back toward home, as the colored people of Cassange had told them he was leading them down to the coast to sell them, that they would be taken on board a ship, fattened, and eaten— the white people being cannibals. Livingstone

asked if they had ever heard of an Englishman
buying and selling people; if he had not refused
to take the slave offered him by Shinte. But,
said he, "as I have always behaved as an English
teacher, if you now doubt my intentions, you had
better not go to the coast. I expect to meet some
of my countrymen there, and am determined to
go on." They replied that they only thought it
right to tell him what they had heard; but they
did not intend to leave him, and were willing to
follow wherever he should lead them.

Mr. Rego, the commandant, offered a soldier
as guard to Ambaca; and gave Livingstone an
ox and a parting dinner. All the merchants of
Cassange accompanied him to the edge of the
plateau on which the town stands. They were
carried by slaves in hammocks. "We parted,"
Livingstone writes, "with the feeling in my mind
that I should never forget their disinterested
kindness. They not only did every thing they
could to make my men and me comfortable during our stay; but there being no hotels in Loanda, they furnished me with letters of recom-
mendation to their friends in that city, requesting them to receive me into their houses, for
without these a stranger might find himself a
lodger in the streets. May God remember them
in the day of their need!"

The soldier guide, furnished by the commandant, was a black militia corporal. He was a native of Ambaca; and, like most of the inhabitants of that district, could read and write. He
had three slaves, who carried him in a "tipoia,"
or hammock hung to a pole. The slaves being
young, and not strong enough to carry him far
at a time, he was sufficiently considerate to walk
when the company were not near a village.
Whenever they approached one he mounted his
tipoia, and entered the place in state. When
quite out of sight of the village again, he dismounted and relieved his servants. Two slaves
were occupied with carrying his tipoia, and the
other carried a wooden box about three feet long,
which contained clothing, dishes, and writing
materials. When he wanted to make a purchase
at any of the villages, he would sit down, make
a little ink from gunpowder, and write a note to
the shop-keeper, asking the price, addressing him
by the pompous title, "Illustrissimo Senhor"—
Most Illustrious Sir. This is the usual mode of
address throughout Angola. An answer would
be returned in the same style. If this was satisfactory, another note closed the bargain. Some
other traits of this guide were less pleasing. He
had far less of honesty and truthfulness than Livingstone's heathen attendants. "A land of slaves

is a bad school for even the free." He would connive with those of whom the company purchased food to cheat them for a share of the plunder. A remedy was at last applied by keeping him at a distance from the place where they were bargaining. He took them safely down to Ambaca, however; and Livingstone was pleased to find, on his return to Cassange, that the corporal had been promoted to the position of sergeant-major of a company of militia.

At the village of Tala Mungongo a house was furnished the travelers to sleep in. Here and at other Portuguese stations through this country, travelers' houses have been provided, after the fashion of the khans or caravansaries of the East. They are built of interwoven branches, and plastered with mud. They contain benches of poles, for the bed of the traveler to rest upon, a table, chairs, and a large jar of water. A few miles from this village is the mountain from which it takes its name. The ascent is steep and slippery—a narrow path running along between deep gorges. Livingstone accomplished the ascent in an hour, and found himself upon a broad table land, among lofty trees. One of these, named Mononga-zambi, bears a fruit about the size of a thirty-two-pound shot.

Passing through a fertile and well-populated

country, our company rested on Sunday, the 30th of April, at Ngio, near the ford of the River Quize. Reaching Ambaca, they were politely received by the commandant, Arsenio de Carpo, who spoke a little English. Some ten or twelve miles to the north of this village, the missionary station of Cahenda once stood. The Jesuit and Capuchin missionaries stationed there taught the people, and ever since their expulsion by the Marquis of Pombal, the people have taught each other. As the result, large numbers throughout the district can read and write. The district is said to contain upward of forty thousand inhabitants.

It was the 24th of May when they reached Golungo Alto. This is Winter in this country. The thermometer stands at 80° in day-time, and sinks to 76° at night. The green hills surrounding the place are cultivated up to the top with manioc, coffee, cotton, ground-nuts, bananas, pine-apples, pitangas, guavas, papaws, custard-apples, and jambos—fruits which had been brought from South America by the missionaries. All kinds of fruit-trees and grape-vines bear fruit twice a year, with very little labor, and without irrigation. Grains and vegetables produce two crops. At Trombeta a fine coffee plantation was seen, belonging to the sub-commandant, residing here.

The grounds around his house were laid out with taste, and decorated with flowers. Rows of trees were planted along each side of the road, with flowers and pine-apples interspersed. This was the first display of real taste in such matters which had been seen since they left the hospitable mansion of Mozinkwa, in Loanda. This gentleman had a fine estate. When a forest, a few years ago, it cost him eighty dollars. Now he has upon it nine hundred coffee trees, which, doubtless, yield him annually sixty times the original investment. These coffee trees begin to yield in three years from the planting, and reach their maximum in six. Cotton was standing in the pods in the field, the proprietor seeming not to care for it.

As they drew near the coast, Livingstone's companions began to look at matters in a very serious light. One asked if they would all have the opportunity of watching each other at Loanda. "Suppose one went for water, would the other see if he were kidnapped?" "I see what you are driving at," was the reply, "and if you suspect me, you may return, for I am as ignorant of Loanda as you are; but nothing will happen to you but what happens to myself. We have stood by each other hitherto, and will do so to the last."

On reaching the elevated plains adjacent to Loanda, they caught their first view of the sea.

The natives looked with astonishment and awe upon the boundless ocean. In describing their feelings afterward they said : "We marched along with our father, believing that what the ancients had told us was true, that the world has no end ; but all at once the world said to us, 'I am finished, there is no more of me !'" They had always thought the world was a plain extended without limit. Mr. Gabriel, the English commissioner for the suppression of the slave-trade, residing at Loanda, had sent an invitation to Livingstone to take up his abode with him, upon arrival at the place. But the message had missed him on the road. He went, however, to the house of this gentleman, not knowing what kind of a reception might greet him. But on reaching his porch, numerous flowers, carefully cultivated, which he saw, led him to infer that the proprietor of the mansion was what he soon found him to be, a real whole-hearted Englishman.

Being ill, the worn and wasted traveler accepted the bed which was kindly offered. "Never," said he, "shall I forget the luxurious pleasure I enjoyed in feeling myself again on a good English couch, after six months sleeping on the ground." He was soon sound asleep. Hoping that the generous hospitality of Mr. Gabriel would soon restore his health, Livingstone remained under his roof. But his disease having been produced by long exposure to malaria, he grew worse even while resting. Several Portuguese gentlemen called upon him soon after his arrival. The Bishop of Angola, the Right Reverend Joaquim Morcira Reis, the acting-governor of the province, sent his secretary to visit him, and offer the services of the government physician. Some British cruising ships came into port, and, in view of Livingstone's emaciated condition, offered to convey him to St. Helena, or homeward. But he felt under obligation to return with his Makololo friends, since his experience of the hostility of the border tribes made it probable they would not get back alive if left to return alone. So he declined the tempting offer of his friends of the English navy. Finding, too, by his journey, that the great amount of rivers, forests, and marsh, in the route he had traveled, would make it impracticable to construct a wagon road through that country, so as to open up the country of Sekeletu for trade, he now determined to go back and find a path from that region to the east coast, by means of the great river Zambesi, or Leeambye.

He was glad, however, to avail himself of the medical aid of the Surgeon of the ship "Polyphemus," it having been kindly suggested by the Commander, Captain Phillips.

The medical skill of Mr. Cockin, the surgeon, and the unwearied hospitality of Mr. Gabriel, together with the exhilarating presence of the warm-hearted naval officers, soon worked an improvement in his health. In about two weeks after his arrival he had sufficiently recovered to call on the Bishop. His party of native men accompanied him, arrayed in new robes of striped cotton and red caps, the gift of Mr. Gabriel. The Bishop, now acting as Governor, received them in the great hall of the palace. He asked many very intelligent questions about the Makololo, and gave them permission to come to Loanda as often as they wished. They were delighted with the interview.

The Makololo were very serious in their deportment. They saw many things new and exceedingly strange to them. They looked with awe upon the large stone churches and houses in the vicinity of the ocean. They never could comprehend a two-story house till now. In talking to them about it Livingstone had always been obliged to use the word hut. Their huts are made of poles thrust into the ground; and they could not comprehend how the poles of one hut could be planted on the roof of another, or how men could live in the upper story with the conical roof of the lower hut in the middle.

Some Makololo who had visited Livingstone's house at Kolobeng, in describing it to their countrymen at Linyanti, said, "It is not a hut, it is a mountain with several caves in it."

Commander Bedingfeld and Captain Skene invited them to visit their vessels, the "Pluto" and "Philomel." In view of their fears, Livingstone told them no one need go who had any suspicions of unfair play. But nearly the whole party went. When they were all on the deck of the vessel, Livingstone pointed to the sailors and told the natives, "Now, these are all my countrymen, sent by our Queen for the purpose of putting down the trade of those that buy and sell black men." They replied, "Truly, they are just like you." All their fears seemed to vanish. They went forward among the jolly tars, who, acting very much as the Makololo would do in similar circumstances, offered them bread and beef, of which they were making their dinner. The Commander permitted them to fire off a cannon. Having the highest notions of its power, they were much pleased when Livingstone told them "that is what they put down the slave-trade with." They were filled with amazement at the size of a brig-of-war, and said, "It is not a canoe at all, it is a town." They called the sailors' deck "the kotla," and capped

the climax in their description of this great ark
by saying, "And what sort of a town is it that
you must climb up into with a rope?"

The politeness shown them by the officers and
men had a beneficial effect upon their minds.
Livingstone had been treated with great kindness by them; but now he rose very rapidly in
their estimation when they saw the respect shown
him by his own countrymen. They treated him
with the greatest deference ever afterward.

Wishing to show them a place of worship,
Livingstone took them to the Cathedral when
mass was celebrated. But the gorgeous ritual—
which some think better suited to inspire feelings of reverence and devotion than the simple
forms of Protestant worship—did not produce
any such effect on the minds of these uncul-
tured sons of Nature. The numerous genu-
flexions, changes of position by the priests, their
backs turned to the people, burning incense, the
laughing, talking, and manifest irreverence of the
singers, the firing of guns, etc., failed to inspire
them with any feeling of adoration. In speaking
of it afterward they said "they had seen the
white man charming their demons"—the identical language they used with reference to the
practice of the Balonda in beating drums before
their idols.

In the early part of August Livingstone was afflicted with a relapse, which transformed him to a skeleton. For a considerable time he was unable to give any attention to his men. But, without any prompting, they had established a brisk trade in fire-wood. They started early in the morning, and by daylight reached the uncultivated country surrounding the city. Here they gathered fire-wood, which they brought in and sold to the inhabitants ; and, as they gave larger quantities than the regular wood-carriers, they found a ready sale for all they brought.

A ship loaded with coal for the naval vessels having arrived from England, Mr. Gabriel procured them employment in unloading her at sixpence a day. This occupied them for upward of a month. They were filled with astonishment at the amount of cargo which one ship contained. They expressed their wonder afterward by saying, "We labored fast as possible, every day, from sunrise to sunset, for a moon and a half, unloading stones that burn, and were tired out, still leaving plenty in the ship."

With the money obtained in this way they bought clothing, beads, and other articles to take back to their own country. Their idea of the value of different kinds of goods surprised those who had been accustomed to trade with the natives near the coast. Hearing some persons state confidently that the Africans chose the thinnest fabrics—if they only had gaudy colors, and a large extent of surface—Livingstone questioned the statement, and, in proof of his own opinion, took the Makololo to the store of Mr. Schut to test their judgment in the selection of goods. When they were shown the amount of goods they could buy for a single tusk, they were requested, without any reasons being given, to point out the fabrics they thought most desirable. Then they all at once selected the strongest pieces of English calico, and other goods, showing that they had regard to strength and durability, and not to color. Livingstone believed, from his acquaintance with them, that most of the Bechuanas would have done the same. But he was assured that the natives near the coast, with whom the Portuguese were trading, had less regard to durability. This, perhaps, results from the fact that calico is, among them, the chief circulating medium. Hence, quantity is more important than quality.

During his illness, Livingstone was visited by messengers from the Bishop, who were sent to inquire for his health. Soon as he was able to walk, he went to express his thanks for these civilities. The Bishop's conversation showed him to be a man of great benevolence and kindness of heart. He said he was a Catholic from conviction, but, though he regretted to see others, like his present visitor, pursuing another path, he cherished no uncharitable feelings, and would never sanction any measures of persecution. He compared the different sects of Christians to persons passing down different streets of the city to one of the churches—all would arrive at the same point at last. His good influence in the city and adjacent country is universally acknowledged. He promoted the establishment of schools, which, though more monastic in character than Protestants would like, yet will doubtless be of great advantage to the country. His influence upon the state of morals in the country was good, especially in leading men to abandon the system of concubinage, which prevailed for Christian marriage.

The city of St. Paul de Loanda contains a population of about twelve thousand, the larger part of whom are people of color. It has now very greatly declined from its former magnificence. Various evidences of this are seen throughout the city. A fine cathedral, once a Jesuit college, is now degraded to a workshop. Oxen were seen feeding within the stately walls of another. Shade trees are planted over the

town.   It presents an imposing appearance from
the sea.   It is provided with an effective police,
and a well-managed custom-house.   There are
three forts, in a good state of repair.   The Portuguese authorities are polite and obliging ; " and
if ever any inconvenience is felt by strangers
visiting the port, it must be considered the fault
of the system, and not of the men."

The harbor is formed by the low, sandy island
of Loanda.   The ships ride in safety between
this island and the main land, on which the city
is built.   Part of the island is so low that high,
south-west winds dash the waves over it, and
gradually fill the harbor with sand.   Great quantities of soil are washed down from the hights
above the city during the rainy season, so that
the port near the custom-house, which once contained sufficient water to float the largest ships,
is now dry, at low water.   Hence the ships
anchor a mile north of their former station.

The island is occupied by about thirteen hundred inhabitants, six hundred of whom are industrious fishermen, and furnish the city daily with
an abundant supply of good fish.

There is not a single English merchant in
the city, and only two American.   Livingstone
thought the arrangements of the custom-house
had some influence in preventing English trade.

Ships coming into the port must be consigned to some one here. The consignee receives one hundred dollars per mast, and a per centage for boats, and men hired for loading and unloading, and, likewise, on every item that passes through his hands. The port charges, too, are heavy. The Secretary of the Government demands a perquisite of twenty dollars. The chief physician must have a fee, with something for the hospital, custom-house officers, guards, etc. Still, our countrymen carry on a very brisk and lucrative trade in calico, biscuit, flour, and butter.

It was the opinion of Livingstone that the home Government of the Portuguese has not usually received as much credit as was due for its sincerity in efforts to suppress the slave-trade. Mr. Gabriel stated that he saw, in 1839, no less than thirty-seven slaveships lying in this harbor, under the protection of the guns of the fort, waiting for their cargoes of human freight. A certain sum per head was paid the Government for all the slaves exported. And the revenue from this source exceeded that derived from all the rest of the commerce. Thus it appears that the Government, in agreeing to the suppression of that traffic, actually sacrificed the chief part of the export revenue. Since that time, however, the revenue from lawful commerce has

grown so as greatly to exceed that formerly derived from the slave-trade.

A brief statement of the objects had in view
by Livingstone in opening up the country, which
was published in the newspapers of Angola, very
much interested the merchants and General Government at Loanda. The Board of Public Works,
at the instance of his excellency, the Bishop,
granted a handsome present for Sekeletu, consisting of a horse, a colonel's complete uniform,
and suits of clothing for each of the men who
came with Livingstone. The merchants, also,
by public subscription, made a present of handsome specimens of all their articles of trade,
with two donkeys, designed to introduce the
stock into the country, as these hardy animals
are proof against the tsetse. The presents were
accompanied by letters from the Bishop and the
merchants. They generously gave Livingstone
letters of commendation to the Portuguese authorities in Eastern Africa.

On the 20th of September, 1854, our great
explorer left Loanda, having spent nearly four
months here. His men had accumulated so
many goods of their own that they were unable
to carry his luggage. So the good Bishop furnished him twenty carriers, and sent orders to
all the commandants of districts, through which

he was to pass, to render him all possible assistance. Having been supplied with a new tent by his friends on board the Philomel, he sailed with them to the mouth of the Bengo River. He ascended this river through the district in which the ruined convent of St. Antonio stands. He visited, on this route, a large sugar manufactory owned by a lady, Donna Anna de Sousa. The flat, alluvial lands along this river are well adapted to the cultivation of sugar-cane. This lady had a large number of slaves; but the establishment was far less flourishing than those afterward seen carried on by free labor. In the hope that it may meet the eye of Donna Anna, Livingstone mentions the fact that Mauritius, a man of color, with not one-tenth the number of hands, and with soil not so good, but with free labor, had cleared $25,000 by a single crop.

Reaching the river Lucalla, our traveler sailed down it in a canoe to Massango, accompanied by the Commandant of Cazengo. The river is about eighty-five yards wide, and navigable for canoes from the confluence of the Coanza to about six miles above the mouth of Leimha. Near this point are the massive ruins of an iron foundery, erected by the order of the Marquis of Pombal in 1768. The buildings are of stone, cemented with oil and lime. The dam for water-power, made of the same materials, was twenty-seven feet high. It had been partly broken down by a flood; solid blocks of stone, many yards in length, being carried down the stream. A party of native smiths and miners is kept here in the employ of the Government. They produce from 400 to 500 bars of good malleable iron every month.

The banks of the Lucalla are beautiful. They are thickly planted with orange trees, bananas, and the palm which yields the palm-oil of commerce. Native houses, with little boys and girls playing around them, are seen embowered in shady groves, with large plantations of maize, tobacco, manioc around them. Many climbing plants run up the lofty cotton, silk, and baobal trees, hanging their beautiful flowers in gay festoons on the branches. The soil is very fertile.

In the town of Massango, which has something more than a thousand inhabitants, there are the ruins of two churches, a hospital, and two convents. There is neither priest nor schoolmaster in the place; but some of the children were taught by one of the inhabitants. The fort is small, but in good repair. It contains some very ancient guns. They are breech-loading, and must have been formidable weapons in their time. The natives have a remarkable fear of cannon. This contributes to the stability of the Portuguese authority.

Returning up the Lucalla, several flourishing coffee plantations were visited. Mr. Pinto, the gentlemanly proprietor of one of these, generously gave Livingstone a liberal supply of excellent coffee, and presented his men with a pair of rabbits to carry into their country. The women were seen employed in spinning cotton, and cultivating their lands. Their only implement for this work is a double-handled hoe, which is worked with a sort of dragging motion. Some of the men were engaged in weaving. A web, which it requires a month to finish, brings them only two shillings.

Some of the men had been left to rest from their travel at Golungo Alto, and, on returning, Livingstone found several of them sick with fever. One of them had an attack of insanity. He came to his comrades, one day, and said, "Remain well. I am called away by the gods!" and off he ran at the top of his speed. The young men gave chase, and caught him before he had run a mile, and bound him. By gentle treatment he recovered in a few days. Livingstone saw several instances of this kind, but he was led to think continued insanity and idiocy extremely rare.

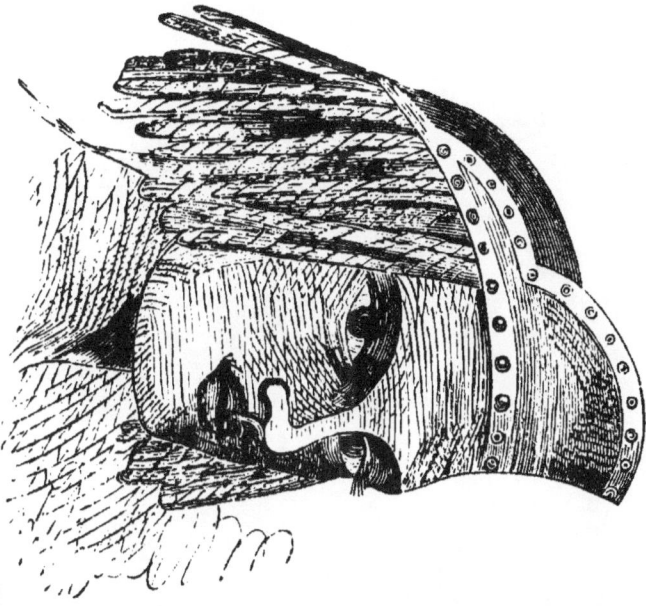

TATTOOING AND HAIR-DRESSING.

The principal recreations of the natives of Angola are weddings and funerals. When a young woman is about to be married, she is anointed with unguents, placed in a hut alone, and numerous incantations are used to secure her good fortune. After some days she is removed to another hut, and dressed in the richest clothing, and finest ornaments her friends can lend or borrow. Then she is placed in some public situation, and saluted as a lady, presents from all her acquaintances being placed around her; then she is taken to the residence of her husband, where she has a hut for herself, and becomes one of several wives—for polygamy prevails here. The occasion is celebrated for several days with dancing, feasting, and drinking. In case of separation, the woman returns to her own family, and the man receives back from her parents the price he paid for her. For mulattoes, the price is sometimes as high as two hundred and forty dollars. Dear wives, are they not?

When a death occurs the body is kept for several days. A great gathering of both sexes is had, and feasting and debauchery, beating of drums and dancing, are kept up in accordance with the ability of the relatives. The great ambition is to give their friends an expensive funeral. Sometimes these expenses are so heavy that years elapse before they are paid.   On the last day of the ceremonies a pig is slaughtered and eaten, its head being thrown into a stream.   When one is asked to sell a pig, he often replies, " I am keeping it in case of the death of any of my friends." If a native, found intoxicated on such occasion, is blamed for his intemperance, he justifies himself by saying, " Why, my mother is dead !" That he thinks sufficient reason for getting drunk.

These people are very obstinate, and fond of litigation.   A case came before the weekly court of Mr. Canto, the Commandant, involving property in a palm-tree, worth about two pence.   The Judge advised the complainant to withdraw the suit, since the cost of entering it would be more than the whole value of the tree.   " O no," he replied, " I have a piece of calico with me for the clerk, and money for you.   It is my right; I will not forego it."   The calico cost three or four shillings—several times the worth of the property.   They find very great pleasure in being able to say of an enemy, " I took him before the court."

Delayed here by the illness of the horse presented by the Bishop for Sekeletu, Livingstone improved the opportunity to observe a curious insect which inhabits trees of the fig family.

Seven or eight of them cluster around a spot on one of the smaller branches. They keep up a constant distillation of a clear fluid, which drops upon the ground, and forms a little puddle. You may catch three or four pints of the fluid during a night, if you place a vessel under them. The natives say a drop spattered in the eyes produces inflammation. Both the natives and naturalists think the fluid is sucked from the tree. After careful observations and experiments, Livingstone came to the conclusion that the fluid is distilled from the atmosphere, by some mysterious process, of which these insects have the exclusive patent. He tried the following experiment: Finding a colony of these insects at their work of distilling on a branch of the castor oil plant, he stripped off the bark between them and the trunk of the plant for a distance of twenty inches, and scraped off the inner bark, so as to destroy all the vessels of the ascending sap. He then cut a hole in the side of the branch, and cut out the pith and internal vessels. But this cutting off the supplies of moisture furnished by the tree made no difference with these distillers. When the experiment began they were producing one drop each sixty-seven seconds, or about two ounces, five-and-a-half drams, every twenty-four hours. But, as usual, during the night, when there is

more moisture in the air, the process was far
more rapid. Next morning it was found they
had been producing fluid at the rate of twelve
drops per minute—that is, sixteen ounces, or one
pint in twenty-four hours. He then cut the
branch so that it broke during the day, but they
went on with their work at the same rate.

Another colony with which the same form of
experiment was tried, produced a drop every two
seconds, or four pints and ten ounces in twenty-
four hours. There was no perforation of the
branch to be seen where these insects clustered ;
and these experiments make it highly probable,
to say the least, that they do not derive any
moisture from the tree, but, by some peculiar
power they possess, distill it from the air. Still,
they will not remain on a branch entirely severed
from the tree.

On crossing the river Lucalla, a detour to the
south was made for the purpose of visiting the
rocks of Pungo Andongo. A change in the vegetation of the country was soon noticed. There
were trees identical with those which grow south
of the Chobe. The grass stands in tufts, and is
of the kind thought by the natives to be best
adapted for cattle ; and the plump condition of
the cattle shows the effect of rich pasturage.
Livingstone had been uniformly referred to

Pungo Andongo in all his previous inquiries as to the productions of Angola. "Do you grow wheat?" "O yes, in Pungo Andongo." "Grapes, figs, peaches?" "O yes, in Pungo Andongo." "Do you make butter and cheese?" "Abundance in Pungo Andongo." But when he reached the place he found all this referred to the agricultural products of one man, Colonel Manuel Antonio Pires.

The fort of Pungo Andongo is situated in the midst of a singular group of columnar-shaped rocks. Each of them is upward of three hundred feet high. They are composed of conglomerate, made up of a variety of rounded pieces of rock, in a matrix of dark-red sandstone, and rest on a thick stratum of this rock. These gigantic pillars seem to have been formed by a current of the sea coming from the south-east, ages ago, when the relations of land and sea were altogether different from what they now are. The pieces imbedded in the conglomerate are gneiss, clay shale, mica, and sandstone schists, trap, and porphyry. Most of these are large enough to give the whole the appearance of being the only remaining vestiges of vast primeval banks of shingle. Several little streams wind around among the rocks. The village is completely environed by them, and the pathways leading to it might easily be defended by a small body of troops against an army. This was the stronghold of the original inhabitants of the country, the Jinga.

A footprint carved upon one of these rocks was shown Livingstone, and is said to be that of a famous Queen, who reigned over all this region. The history of Angola tells of the famous Queen, Donna Anna de Sowzga, who came from this vicinity to Loanda, in 1621, as an embassadress for her brother, Gola Bandy, king of the Jinga. She came to sue for peace, and surprised the Governor by the promptness of her answers. The Governor proposed the payment of tribute annually by the Jinga as a condition of peace. She at once replied, "People talk of tribute when they have conquered, and not before; we come to talk of peace, not of subjection." She gained all she sought, remained some time in Loanda, was taught by the missionaries, and baptized in the Catholic faith. She returned to her own country with honor, and succeeded to the kingdom at the death of her brother, whom she was suspected of poisoning. In a subsequent war with the Portuguese, she lost, in a great battle, nearly all her army. After a long apostasy she returned to the Church, and died at a very great age.

CHAPTER IX.

An Alligator with a Slave Boy—A Native Diviner—An
African Wake—Beauty of Scenery and Climate—A
Blow on the Beard—The Kasendi—Hostile Natives—
Encounter with a Buffalo—Return to Linyanti.

Colonel Pires, whose generous hospitality
Livingstone was now enjoying, came to this
country as a servant on a ship. By persevering
industry he has become the richest merchant in
the district of Angola. He owns thousands of
cattle, and, in any emergency, can take the field
at the head of an army of several hundred well-
armed slaves. His slaves appeared more like free
servants than is usual in such establishments.
Instead of that negligence and slovenliness, usually seen, which indicates the disposition to do as
little for the master as possible, every thing here
was neat and clean, as though the servants took
a real interest and pride in the establishment.

The mansion of the Colonel is outside the
rocks, and commands a magnificent view of the
surrounding country. He had another estate on
the banks of the Coanza, about six miles distant,

which Livingstone visited once a week with him
for the sake of recreation.

The difference in temperature between these
two places was such that the cashew trees were
just coming into flower at the estate near the
rocks, while on the lower land, by the river, they
were ripening their fruit. Cocoanut and banana
trees bear well at the lower plantation, while at
the other they yield but little fruit.   The difference of temperature indicated by the thermometer was 7°.   The general range at the rocks
was 67° at seven o'clock in the morning ; 74° at
noon ; and 72° in the evening.   This was in the
month of December.

A slave boy belonging to the Colonel having
stolen some melons and eaten them, went to the
river to wash his mouth, so as not to be detected
by the flavor upon his breath.   An alligator undertook to punish him for the theft, and seized
him and carried him to an island in the middle
of the river.   Here the poor fellow caught hold
of some reeds and held them so firmly as to baf-
fle all the efforts of the reptile to dislodge him.
His cries attracted the attention of his companions, and they came in a canoe to his assistance.
The alligator at once let go his hold when they
appeared, and the boy was saved.   He had, however, many marks of the ugly reptile's teeth upon

his thigh and body, and of his claws upon the legs and arms.

A large number of ancient burial-places are seen in this vicinity, where the Jinga have buried their dead. They are large mounds of stone, with cooking vessels of rude pottery placed upon them. Some of the mounds are in a circular form, shaped like a haycock, and two or three yards in diameter. The natives of Angola bury their dead at the side of the most frequented paths. They are especially anxious to secure for that purpose the point where cross-roads meet. They place water-bottles, broken pipes, cooking vessels, and, sometimes, a little bow and arrow on the grave; and plant upon and around it tree euphorbias, and other species of that family. The Portuguese Government have tried in vain to break up this custom of burying in the roads by penalties, and by appointing places of burial in each district. But, in spite of the most rigid enforcement of the law, the natives follow their ancient custom.

Notwithstanding the fertility of the soil, the people of Angola do but little in the way of agriculture. No plow is used. All cultivation is performed with the native hoe, in the hands of slaves. The half-breed Portuguese have less energy than their fathers. The staple product is manioc, which does not afford sufficient nutriment to give stamina to the people. This plant bears drought, without the leaves shriveling, as other plants do when deprived of rain. The leaves make an excellent vegetable for the table. The stalk makes good fuel, and affords a large amount of potash. In alluvial soils, when well watered, it matures in ten or twelve months. Tapioca is made from the root, by rasping it when raw, placing it upon a cloth, and pouring water upon it while rubbing it with the hands. It parts with its starchy, glutinous matter. This, when it settles in the bottom of the vessel, and the water is poured off, is placed in the sun till nearly dry. The drying is completed on an iron plate, over a slow fire, the mass being stirred, meanwhile, with a stick. In the interior of Angola, fine manioc meal, which is easily convertible into superior starch, or the tapioca of commerce, is sold at the rate of ten pounds for a penny. There is, however, no other means of transportation to Loanda than the shoulders of carriers and slaves, over a foot-path.

The King of Congo, whose dominions are north of Angola, is said to be a Christian. And it is stated there are no less than twelve churches in the Kingdom, as the result of a mission formerly established at the Capitol, San Salvador.

When a King of Congo dies, the body is wrapped in many folds of cloth, and kept till a priest can come from Loanda and consecrate his successor. No priests live now in the interior of the country, probably on account of the prevalence of fever. The King of Congo retains the title, Lord of Angola, which he possessed when the original inhabitants of that country, the Jinga, owed him allegiance. When he writes to the Governor of Angola he places his own name first, as though he were addressing a vassal.

During his stay at Pungo Andongo, Livingstone was employed in reproducing some papers, dispatches, maps, etc., which had been lost on the mail packet, Forerunner, of the loss of which he had just heard. But this unwelcome news was coupled with the grateful intelligence that his friend, Lieutenant Bedingfield, who had them in charge, had escaped the imminent peril to which he had been exposed—of going to the bottom of the sea with them.

Livingstone left Pungo Andongo on the first of January, 1855. Just before reaching Cassange he was overtaken by the Commandant, who, with a detachment of fifty men and a cannon, was returning from an unsuccessful search for a party of rebels. Senhor Carvalho, the Commandant, invited him to partake of his hospitality, but he declined, wishing to call on Captain Neves, whose kindness he had shared when he first arrived in the Portuguese possessions. A child of his generous host died during this visit. His mother, a colored woman, sent for a diviner during the child's illness, to learn from him what was best to be done. This functionary came, and, after throwing his dice, he worked himself into the frenzy or ecstasy in which they pretend to have communication with the Barimo, or disembodied spirits. He then gave oracular response that the child was being killed by the spirit of a Portuguese trader, who had formerly lived at Cassange. At the death of this trader the merchants of the village took his goods, and, dividing them among each other, rendered account of the portion each received to his creditors at Loanda. The natives who looked on upon these transactions and were utterly ignorant of written mercantile operations, thought the merchants had stolen the goods of the trader; and, as Captain Neves had taken part in the affair, they supposed the spirit of the trader was now taking revenge by killing the Captain's boy. The mother urged the father to give a slave to the diviner as a fee, so that he might propitiate the spirit by sacrifice. But the father quietly called in a neighbor, and they applied a couple of sticks to the back of the diviner, which quickly broke the spell, and brought him to his senses, when he fled precipitately.

The mother of the sick child seemed to have no confidence in civilized wisdom, and refused to obey the directions of Dr. Livingstone in his treatment. She had him cupped on the cheeks, and the poor little fellow was soon in a dying state. At the request of the father, the dying boy was baptized by the missionary, and his soul commended to the care and mercy of him who said, "Of such is the kingdom of heaven." The mother at once ran away, and began a touching, doleful wail, expressive of hopeless sorrow. This was continued till the child died. In the evening her female companions came and used a screeching musical instrument as an accompaniment to the death wail.

Association with the whites does not seem to have improved the condition of the natives here very greatly. In the different districts of Angola, many persons are said to be sacrificed to the cruel superstitions of the country, without any interference of the Portuguese authorities.

Persons accused of witchcraft are subjected to an ordeal which usually results in their death. The accused person will often come from distant districts to brave the test and prove her innocence. They come to the river Dua, on the Cassange, and drink the infusion of a poisonous tree, and perish unknown. The poison is very virulent. When a strong stomach throws it off, the charge is reiterated, and the dose repeated, and the victim dies. Hundreds perish in this way every year. Those who administer the ordeal bind the natives to secrecy.

These superstitions are the same as those which prevail throughout the country north of the Lyambesi. This has been thought to indicate a common origin of the people. They all believe that the spirits of the departed mingle still among the living, and partake of their food. In sickness, sacrifices of fowls and goats are offered to propitiate the spirits. One man who kills another, offers a sacrifice to lay the spirit of his victim. The existence of a sect is reported who kill men in order to offer their hearts to the Barimo.

The merchants of Cassange carry on a considerable trade with the surrounding country by means of native traders, called Pombeiros. Two of these, Pedro Joa Baptista and Antonio Jose, called in the history of Angola "trading blacks," actually crossed the continent in the year 1815— the only instance of such an achievement by native Portuguese subjects. No European had ever accomplished it at this time. And this hero missionary, whose footprints we are following, has the honor of being the first white man to perform the task. .

Before reaching the river Quango our party was brought to a halt by the sickness of two of their number, who were attacked with fever. They stopped near the residence of a Portuguese who rejoiced in the name of William Tell. He lived here in spite of the prohibition of the Government. This gentleman came to invite Livingstone to dinner, and he drank a little of the water they were using from a pond. This gave him fever, showing how great was the exposure of these travelers. Traveling in the sun, with the thermometer from 96° to 98° in the shade, produced great thirst, and they were obliged to drink any water they could find.

The Makololo men were busily engaged in collecting fowls and pigeons to improve the breed of their own country. Mr. Tell presented them with some fine, large specimens from Rio Janeiro, of which they were remarkably proud. They carried them in triumph through the Balonda country as evidence of having been to the sea. But, very much to their sorrow, the giant of the whole flock of eighty-four was selected and carried off by a hungry hyena in search of supper, while the whole party were fast asleep, at the village of Shinte. These Makololo, who were so anxious to improve the breed of their domestic animals, thought the Portuguese must be an inferior race of white men, because they kept only the native cattle, made no use of the milk, and slaughtered indiscriminately their cows and heifer calves, which these natives never do.

They were constantly talking of the fine soil for gardens, over which they were passing. When Livingstone casually remarked that most of the flour used by the Portuguese came from another country, they exclaimed, "Are they ignorant of tillage?" "They know nothing but buying and selling; they are not men." As he wrote these remarks of the Makololo, Livingstone wished they might reach the ears of his Angolese friends, and stir them up to develop the resources of their fine and fertile country.

On returning to the village of Cypriano, the travelers found his step-father had died, and, in accordance with the custom of the country, he had spent more than his patrimony in funeral ceremonies. He was kind and generous as before; but his drinking habits had got him so deeply in debt that he was obliged to shun his creditors.

A death had just occurred in a village about a

mile distant, and the people were busily engaged
in beating drums and firing guns. Their funeral
orgies somewhat resembles an Irish wake—half
festive and half mourning. Nothing can be more
heart-rending than their death wails. Whenever
these people look to the future world, they have
only the most gloomy view of their own utter
helplessness, and their hopeless condition. They
think themselves entirely in the power of disembodied spirits. Hence, they are constantly dep-
recating their wrath, and trying to appease them.
They think there is no other cause of death, except witchcraft, which may be averted by charms.
The whole colored population of Angola are under the influence of these gross superstitions.
But for these they might enjoy life very highly.
They have a splendid climate, and a luxuriant
country. Upon this subject the words of Livingstone must be quoted. "I have often thought,
in traveling through their land, that it presents
pictures of beauty which angels might enjoy.
How often have I beheld, in still mornings,
scenes the very essence of beauty, and all bathed
in a quiet air of delicious warmth! yet the
occasional soft motion imparting a pleasing sen-
sation of coolness as of a fan. Green, grassy
meadows, the cattle feeding, the goats browsing,
the kids skipping, the groups of herd-boys with

bows, arrows, and spears; the women wending their way to the river with water-pots poised jauntily on their heads; men sewing under the shady banians; and old, gray-headed fathers sitting on the ground, with staff in hand, listening to the morning gossip, while others carry trees or branches to repair their hedges; and all this flooded with the bright, African sunshine, and the birds singing among the branches before the heat of the day has become intense, form pictures which never can be forgotten."

Reaching the river Quango, the ferryman demanded thirty yards of calico for toll, but he finally received six thankfully. The canoes were wretched, conveying only two persons across at a time. The men, however, were quite at home in the water, and the party were all over in about two hours and a half. Their dexterity in managing the cattle and donkeys were the admiration of the people, who were looking on. The proverbial stubbornness of the donkey was of little account in this case. He was utterly powerless in the hands of these men. Five or six of them would seize one of the beasts and tumble him into the river, and thus force him to swim over. Some of the men swam along by the cattle, and drove them on by dashing water at their heads.

The travelers did not visit their friend of the conical head-dress, who had annoyed them so much on their coastward journey, but passed on to the residence of some Ambakistas, or natives of Ambaca, who had crossed the river in order to secure the first chances of trade in bees-wax. These people are noted for their fondness for knowledge. The history of Portugal, Portuguese law, and all kinds of learning, within their reach, are studied with eagerness. They write a fine, lady-like hand, very highly esteemed by the Portuguese. They are largely employed as clerks and penmen. They are very shrewd in trade, and have been called the Jews of Angola.

Exposure to sun and rain brought Livingstone down again with fever. This was the most severe attack he had suffered. For eight days he lay groaning and tossing with intense pain in the head, quite oblivious to every thing outside of his little tent. But every thing was safe in the care of his trusty attendants. By this illness they were detained twenty-two days. While the head man of the village, near which they were stopping, was bargaining and quarreling for a piece of meat in their camp, it happened that one of the men struck him on the mouth. Livingstone's principal men paid five pieces of cloth and a gun as an atonement; but he became more exorbitant in his demands, the more they yielded. He sent messengers to the surrounding villages to assist him in avenging the affront of a *blow on the beard*. Knowing the courage of these people usually rises with success, Livingstone determined to yield no more, and took his departure. As they were passing through a forest a little way from the village, they were startled by a body of men rushing after them. The burdens of the servants in the rear of the party were thrown down, and several shots were fired; but the trees were so thick no one was harmed by the firing. After Livingstone's departure from Loanda, Captain Henry Reed, of Her Majesty's brig, "Linnet," had sent him a six-barreled revolver, which reached him at Golungo Alto. Forgetting his fever, he seized this and staggered rapidly along the path, with two or three of his men, toward the assailants. When he encountered the chief, the sight of the six-shooter pointing at his breast, and the ghastly visage of the sick man, produced a very sudden revolution in his martial feelings. He exclaimed, "O I have only come to speak with you, and wish peace only." His gun was examined and found empty. Both parties now crowded up to their chiefs. One of the assailants, coming too near, one of Livingstone's men drove him back

with his battle-ax. They protested their peaceable intentions. But the fact of their having
knocked down the goods was urged as proof to
the contrary.

Livingstone now requested all to sit down;
and Pitsane quieted their fears by placing his
hand upon the muzzle of the revolver. The missionary then said to the chief: "If you have
come with peaceable intentions, we have no
other; go away home to your village." He replied, "I am afraid lest you shoot me in the
back." "If I wanted to kill you," said Livingstone, "I could shoot you in the face as well."
Mosantu called out, "That's only a Makaloka
trick; do n't give him your back." "Tell him to
observe that I am not afraid of him," said Livingstone, and mounted his ox. The villagers expected, by their sudden attack, to frighten the
travelers away from their goods, and thus plunder them easily.

The assaulting party were, in the issue of the
affair, very glad to get away unharmed; and the
travelers, too, were glad to get off without shedding blood, or compromising themselves in any
way that might prove unpleasant in case of a further visit to this part of the country. The mer
were delighted with their own bravery, and made
the woods ring with eloquent descriptions of

the "brilliant conduct before the enemy" if the hostilities had not ceased so soon.

Livingstone was so feeble he was glad to avail himself of the company of Senhor Pascoal and other native traders, who were traveling for some distance on the same route with him. One of these Pombeiros, or traders, had eight good-looking women chained together, whom he was taking to the country of Matiamvo, to sell for ivory. They were probably captives taken from the rebel Cassanges.

Reaching the Loajima on the 30th of April, they were obliged to construct a bridge to cross the river. This task, however, was soon accomplished. Senhor Pascoal found a tree growing in a horizontal position, and it reaching partly across, they soon constructed a bridge of ropes made from the tough, climbing plants which abound in the country. The stream was about twenty-five yards wide at this point. The people in this region are more slender in form, and of lighter olive color than any seen elsewhere. The mode of dressing the hair, adopted by them, and their general features, reminded Livingstone of the ancient Egyptians. A few of the ladies attach the hair to a hoop, which encircles the head. Others wear an ornament of woven hair and hide, decorated with beads, sometimes adding the tails of buffaloes. Others still, weave their own hair on pieces of hide, and give them the form of buffaloes' horns, or make a single horn in front. Some of them tattoo their bodies by inserting some black substances beneath the skin, which makes an elevated cicatrix half an inch in length. These figures are sometimes in the form of stars.

At the village of Nyakalonga, the travelers were handsomely treated by a sister of the late Matiamvo. She desired her people to guide them to the next village; but they declined to do this, unless the party would engage in trade with them. She, however, sent her son without requiring payment. She asked them to wait an hour or two, till she could get ready a present of manioc, roots, meal, ground-nuts, and a fowl. After the opposite experiences lately met with on the path of the slave-traders, these civilities were very pleasant.

On the 2d of June our company halted for the night at the village of Kawawa, who is a man of some importance in this country. The village is surrounded by a forest, and consists of forty or fifty huts. Drums were beating over the body of a man who had died the day before, and the hubbub continued all night long. Some women were making a clamorous wail at the door of the

hut where the man had died, and talking to him
as though he were living. A person fantastically
dressed, with a great number of feathers, representing one of the Barimo, left the people at the
wailing and dance, and went away into the deep
forest.

Next morning a very agreeable intercourse
was had with Kawawa; and most of the day
was spent in talking with him and his people.
When his visit was returned, he was found in his
large court-house, which was very well built, and
in the shape of a bee-hive.

A case was brought before him for judgment.
It was that of a poor man and his wife, who were
accused of having bewitched the man whose
wake had just been held in the village. Without waiting to hear a word of the defense, the
chief said, "You have killed one of my children;
bring all yours before me, that I may choose
which of them shall be mine instead." The wife
defended herself with eloquence, but it was of no
avail. These are the means resorted to by these
chiefs to obtain subjects for the slave markets.
In the evening the magic lantern was exhibited.
All were delighted except Kawawa, who manifested fear, and several times attempted to run
away, but was prevented by the crowd. The
more intelligent understood the explanations, and

expatiated upon them eloquently to the obtuse and stupid.

Notwithstanding the great civilities which had passed between them, when Livingstone, on the next morning, sent word to Kawawa that he was ready to start, he replied, in his figurative language, " If an ox come in the way of a man, ought he not to eat it ?" The white man had given an ox to the Chibogue, and must give him the same, with a gun, gunpowder, and a black robe, like that he had seen spread out to dry, the day before. If the ox was refused, he said a man must be given, and a book, by which he might see the heart of Matiamvo, and which would forewarn him if Matiamvo should ever resolve to cut off his head. After sending this message he came to the encampment and said he had seen all the goods of the travelers, and, unless they paid this tribute, he would prevent their passing the Kasai River, which lay before them. Livingstone replied that the goods were his property ; that he would never have it said that a white man paid tribute to a black ; and that he should cross the river in spite of him.

He now gave orders to his people to arm themselves, and when Livingstone's men saw them rushing for their bows, arrows, and spears, they were quite panic-stricken. He ordered them to move on, and not to fire, unless Kawawa's men struck the first blow. But when he started onward, many of his men did not follow. Soon as he discovered this he dismounted from the ox, and rushed toward them with his revolver in hand. Kawawa ran away, and his people showed their backs. He shouted to the men to take up the baggage and march on. All obeyed but one who was preparing to fire on Kawawa, when a punch on the head from Livingstone's pistol prompted him to obey orders, and march on. As they moved off into the forest Kawawa's men stood looking at them, but did not fire a shot or an arrow. Kawawa, we are told, is not a good specimen of the Balonda chiefs ; and it is said he has good reasons to think Matiamvo, who is paramount chief of all this country, will, some time, take off his head for disregarding the rights of strangers.

When they reached the river, about ten miles distant, they found the chief had preceded them by four men, who came with orders to the ferrymen to refuse them passage, unless they gave up the articles that had been mentioned, and one of their men besides. This demand for one of their number always touched every heart. The river was a hundred yards wide, and very deep. The ferrymen asked one of the Batoka if they had rivers in his country, and he answered, truthfully, "No; we have none." Yet, the reader will remember, there were other natives in the company who were very familiar with crossing rivers. When the canoes were taken away the ferrymen thought them entirely unable to cross. Pitsane stood on the bank gazing with a careless air upon the water. He watched the ferrymen carefully, however, and made accurate observation of where the canoes were hidden, in the reeds, and, after it became dark, one of them was borrowed, without consulting the proprietors, and, in a short time, the whole party were nicely bivouacked on the southern bank—the canoe being returned to the side from which it had been taken.

Just as they were ready to start, next morning, Kawawa's people were seen on the opposite bank, amazed to see them across the river, and ready to proceed on their journey. One of them called out, at last, "Ah, ye are bad." To which Pitsane replied, "Ah, ye are good, and we thank you for the loan of your canoe." Livingstone took care to explain the whole affair to Katema and the other chiefs. They all agreed that his conduct was justifiable, and right in the circumstances, and that Matiamvo would approve it. It is the custom of these chiefs to send explanations to each other in this manner, whenever any thing occurs which might bear an unfavorable construction. This prevents their losing character. There is public opinion even among these savages.

Katema and Shinte both welcomed the travelers on their return past their villages, and treated them with great kindness and hospitality. They spent a little time with each of these chiefs. Having reached the Leeba, they descended the river by canoes, some of which they purchased from the Balonda, and others were loaned them by the female chief, Nyamoana, a sister of Shinte. They waited a day, opposite the village of Manenko, and sent a message to her a distance of about fifteen miles from the river. Her husband was at once sent with liberal presents of food, she having a burn on the foot, which rendered her unable to travel.

The next morning Sambanza performed the ceremony called Kasendi, for cementing friendship between the two parties. Sambanza and Pitsane were the principals in the ceremony. They joined hands, and small incisions were made on the clasped hands, on the right cheeks, foreheads, and the pits of the stomach of each. A small quantity of blood was taken from these incisions with a stalk of grass. The blood of one was put into a pot of beer, and of the other in a second pot of beer. Each then drinks the other's blood, and thus they become blood-relations and perpetual friends. During the drinking of the beer, some of the company present ratify the treaty by uttering short sentences, and beating on the ground with clubs.

The principals are now bound to disclose to each other any impending evil. Thus, for example, if Sekeletu should resolve to attack the Balonda, Pitsane would be obliged to inform Sambanza, so that he might escape. And a similar obligation rests upon the other party. They now gave each other the most valuable presents they were able to bestow. Sambanza walked away clothed in Pitsane's suit of green baize, made in Loanda; and Pitsane received two of the highly prized shells, such as Shinte gave Livingstone, and abundant supplies of food.

Livingstone once became blood-relation to a young African woman by accident. She had a large cartilaginous tumor between the bones of the forearm, which she wished him to remove, and, after obtaining the sanction of her husband, he complied with her request. During the operation some blood spurted from one of the small arteries into his eye. As he wiped it out she remarked, "You were a friend before; now you are a blood-relation, and when you pass this way always send me word, that I may cook food for you."

While passing down this river Livingstone had an encounter with a buffalo—one of the most dangerous beasts of the forest. He had shot a zebra, wounding it in the hind leg, and two of his men were pursuing it. While walking slowly over the grassy plain, after the men, he saw a solitary buffalo, which had been disturbed by some of the party, charging upon him at tremendous speed. As he cocked his rifle, with the intention of giving the animal a shot in the forehead when he should come within three or four yards, the thought flashed across his mind, "What if your gun misses fire?" When within about fifteen yards, a small bush and bunch of grass made the buffalo turn a little in his course, so as to expose his shoulder. As the rifle cracked Livingstone fell flat upon his face. The pain made the furious animal suddenly change his purpose of attack, and he bounded past down to the water, where he was found dead. When Livingstone, immediately afterward, in the presence of his men, expressed his thankfulness to God for his escape from this peril, they were very much offended at themselves that they were not near to shield him. The bush near him was a camel thorn, and reminded him that he had returned again to the land of thorns. The country he had just left is one of evergreens.

Reaching the town of Libonta, on the 27th of July, they were received with extravagant demonstrations of joy. They were looked upon as though they had risen from the dead, for the most skillful of the diviners had long ago declared that they had all perished. The women came forth to meet them, with their curious dancing gestures and loud "luliloos." Some carried a mat and stick as a mimic shield and spear. Others rushed forward and kissed the hands and cheeks of their acquaintances in the party. These demonstrations raised such a dust that it was a relief to reach the men gathered in the kotla, and seated in true African dignity and decorum. After numerous expressions of joy, Livingstone arose, thanked them, and explained the causes of their long delay; but left the full report to be made by their own countrymen. He had before been the chief speaker; now he would leave it to them. Pitsane then delivered a speech nearly an hour in length, giving a very flattering picture of the journey, of the kindness of the white men, and of Mr. Gabriel in particular. He said Livingstone had done more than they had expected. He had not only opened up

the path to the other white men, but had concil-
iated the chiefs along the route.

The next day was celebrated as a day of
thanksgiving to God, for bringing them back in
safety to their friends. The men who had been
with the white men decked themselves in their
best clothing—with red caps and white suits.
They tried to imitate the walk of the soldiers
they had seen in Loanda, and called themselves
Livingstone's "braves"—batlabani is their word.
Livingstone spoke to them upon the goodness
of God in preserving the travelers from all their
perils among strange tribes and diseases. A
similar service was held again in the afternoon.

Two oxen were given them for food by the
men, and the women brought abundant supplies
of butter, milk, and meal. This was all a gratuity.
Yet it was cause of regret to Livingstone that
he could make no return. His men explained
the total expenditure of their means. The Li-
bontese very generously replied, "It does not
matter; you have opened up a path for us, and
we shall have sleep."

From quite a distance strangers came flocking
in, most of them bringing presents. These Livingstone distributed among his men. The sickness they had suffered, and many delays, had
exhausted the large stock of goods with which

they had started from Loanda. They returned as poor as when they started; yet no distrust was manifested, and Livingstone's poverty did not diminish his influence. His men said, "Though we return as poor as we went, we have not gone in vain;" and they began at once to gather tusks of hippopotami and other ivory for a second journey. As they passed down the Barotse Valley they were treated with the greatest kindness. An ox was given them at every village, and, sometimes, two were presented them. Livingstone thus expresses his feelings awakened by this kindness: "I felt, and still feel, most deeply grateful, and tried to benefit them in the only way I could—by imparting the knowledge of that Savior who can comfort and supply them in time of need—and my prayer is that he may send his good Spirit to instruct them, and lead them into his kingdom. Even now I earnestly long to return and make some recompense to them for their kindness."

At Naliele, where the party arrived on the 1st of August, they found the chief, Mpololo, in great affliction. His daughter and her infant child had just been murdered by an enemy, who had entered the hut by night, and strangled them. He then tried to burn the hut, but, in attemping to kindle a fire, he awakened a servant, and was thus detected. Both the murderer and his wife were thrown into the river. The wife was punished as an accessory before the fact, "having known of her husband's intentions, and not revealing them."

Many of the wives of Livingstone's men had married other men during their absence of two years. Among the number was Mashnana's wife, who was the mother of two of his children. He put on the appearance of indifference, with respect to the matter, and said, "Why, wives are as plentiful as grass, and I can get another; she may go." But still, he would add, "If I had that fellow I would open his ears for him." Most of the men had more wives than one, and Livingstone tried to console them by telling them they had enough yet, and more than he had. Some, however, had lost, in this way, the only wives they ever had. In these cases, Livingstone asked the chief to restore them.

• Some time before reaching Sesheke, news reached him that a party of Matabele—the people of Mosilikatse—had left some packages of goods, sent him by Mr. Moffat, on the bank of the river near Victoria Falis.

These two tribes are determined enemies of each other, and when the Matabele called to the Makololo, from the south bank of the river,

asking them to come over with canoes and receive the goods sent by Moffat to "Nake"—the
white man—the Makololo replied, "Go along
with you; we know better than that. How
could he tell Moffat to send his goods here, he
having gone away to the north?" The Matabele
answered, "Here are the goods; we leave them
before you, and if you leave them to perish the .
guilt will be yours." The Makololo thought it
was a trick of their enemies to put witchcraft
medicine in all their hands, and thus do them
injury. But, after the Matabele had left, and
after much divination, they at last went over,
and, with fear and trembling, removed the packages to an island in the middle of the river.
They then built a hut over them to protect them
from the weather. And here Livingstone found
them, in perfect safety, where they had been de-
posited for a year. The news was stale which
was found with the packages; but there were
some good eatables sent by Mrs. Moffat. The
words of the great explorer himself must be
given upon one point, of which no one else can
speak so well:

"Among other things I discovered that my
friend, Sir Roderick Murchisson, while in his
study, in London, had arrived at the same conclusion respecting the form of the African conti-

nent as I had lately come to on the spot; and
that from attentive study of the geological map
of Mr. Bain, and other materials, some of which
were furnished by the discoveries of Mr. Oswell
and myself, he had not only clearly enunciated
the peculiar configuration as an hypothesis in his
discourse before the Geographical Society in
1852, but had even the assurance to send me out
a copy for my information! There was not
much use in nursing my chagrin at being thus
fairly cut out by the man who had foretold
the existence of the Australian gold before its
discovery, for here it was in black and white. In
his easy chair he had forestalled me by three
years, though I had been working hard through
jungle, marsh, and fever, and, since the light
dawned on my mind at Dilolo, had been cherish-
ing the pleasing delusion that I should be the
first to suggest the idea that the interior of Africa was a watery plateau of less elevation than
the flanking, hilly ranges."

A few days were spent at Sesheke, waiting for
the horses which had been left at Linyanti.
When the latter place was reached every thing
which had been left there in the care of the
natives—wagon and goods—was found perfectly
safe. A great picho of all the people was called
to hear the report of the journey, and receive the

presents sent by the Governor and merchants of
Loanda. Livingstone stated that these things
were not his property, but were sent as gifts from
the white men to show their friendly feelings, and
their desire to enter into commercial relations
with the Makololo. He then requested his companions to give a true account of what they had
seen. The marvelous things did not lose any
thing in telling. The climax of the whole story
invariably was that the travelers had finished the
whole world, having turned back only when there
was no land. The presents were received with
delight. On Sunday, when Sekeletu, the chief,
entered church in his military uniform, it attracted more attention than the sermon. Livingstone was complimented and flattered constantly. Volunteers offered to accompany him
to the east coast. They wished to be able to
return and relate strange things like his former
companions.

A second picho was called soon after this to
discuss the question of the removal of the tribe to
the Barotse Valley, in order to be nearer the market. Some of the old men did not like to give
up the line of defense afforded by the rivers
Chobe and Lyambesi against their enemies, the
Matabele. And the young men objected because
the grass grows so rank at the Barotse, that they

could not run fast, and because it is never cool there.

Sekeletu at last rose and addressed Livingstone. He said: "I am perfectly satisfied as to the great advantage for trade, of the path which you have opened, and think that we ought to go to the Barotse in order to make the way from us to Loanda shorter; but with whom am I to live there? If you were coming with us I would remove to-morrow; but now, you are going to the white man's country to bring ma Robert, [Mrs. Livingstone,] and when you return you will find me near to the spot on which you wish to dwell."

AMONG THE MONKEYS.

CHAPTER X.

A New Journey Begun—Falls of Victoria—Elephant Hunting—Man Tossed by a Buffalo—Arrival at Killimane—Embarking for England—Insanity of Sekwebu.

The difficulty which the late exploration had shown to lie in the way of opening a wagon road to Loanda, led to plans for a journey to the east coast. And the question now came up as to what part of the coast they should attempt to reach, and by what route. Some Arab traders, now among the Makololo, had come from Lyanzibar through a country of peaceful tribes. They described the population as located in small villages, like the Balonda. They told of three large rivers and a lake filled with islands, which it required three days to cross in canoes. This seemed the safer route, but, as it was desirable to find a permanent water conveyance, the path along the Lyambas was decided upon.

Ben Habib, one of the Arab traders, being about to return to Loanda, asked for the daughter of Sebituane—now about twelve years old—in marriage. The Arabs adopt this plan to gain

influence in the tribes. As Livingstone was a
bosom friend of the chief, he was consulted with
reference to the matter, and objected to her being taken away where they might never see her
again. But the prudent and wily Arab will,
doubtless, renew his suit on some other occasion with success.

Sekeletu was very fond of the sweetened coffee, and dined with Livingstone as long as his
stock of sugar held out. When told how it was
manufactured from the sugar-cane, he was anxious to procure a sugar-mill, and said he would,
in that case, plant large quantities of the cane.
He gave Livingstone an order for a sugar-mill,
a mohair coat, a good rifle, beads, brass wire, and
added, "any other beautiful thing you may see
in your own country." When it was suggested
that a large amount of ivory would be necessary
to execute this commission, both the chief and
his counselors said, "The ivory is all your own;
if you leave any in the country it will be your
own fault."

This new journey was begun on the 3d of November, Livingstone being accompanied for some
distance, at the start, by Sekeletu and about two
hundred of his people. The whole company
were fed at the expense of the chief. To supply them with food he took cattle from every

station they passed on the route. Coming to a
patch of tsetse between Linyanti and Sesheke,
Livingstone and Sekeletu, with about forty of
his young men, waited to pass it by night, while
the rest of the company went forward in day-time.
About ten o'clock at night, during this march,
it became so intensely dark that both horses
and men were completely blinded. The flashes
of lightning spread over the sky in branches like
those of a tree, and eight or ten in number at
one time. The horses trembled and neighed
with fright; and every new flash showed the
men taking different directions, laughing and
stumbling against each other. The thunder
came in louder peals than any other country
than Africa can produce. Then the rain came
down in torrents, and, after the intense heat of
the day, the drenched travelers were soon un-
comfortably cold. Seeing a fire in the distance,
which had been kindled by some other people
journeying along this route, they gladly turned
aside to share its warmth. Livingstone lay down
on the cold ground, expecting to spend an un-
comfortable night—most of his clothing having
gone forward with the rest of the company—
but the chief, Sekeletu, covered the missionary
with his blanket, and lay down himself without
covering. With reference to this generous action

the Doctor says: "I was much affected by this act of genuine kindness. If such men must perish by the advance of civilization, as certain races of animals do before others, it is a pity. God grant that ere this time comes they may receive that Gospel which is a solace for the soul in death!"

Descending the river Chobe about ten miles to Nampéne, at the head of the rapids, the travelers were obliged to leave the canoes and go on foot along the banks of the river. That night they slept opposite the island of Chondo, and crossing the Leknine the next morning, they came to the island of Kalai, formerly the home of Sekote, one of the Bakota chiefs whom Sebituane conquered and drove out from the country. Intending to strike off to the north-east from this point, Livingstone determined to visit the falls of Mosioatunya, more anciently called Shongwe. This first long name seems to have reference to the vapor and the noise produced by the cataract. Without going near them the natives heard the noise of the falls at a distance, and said, with awe, "Mosi oa tunya"—smoke does sound there. The meaning of the word Shongwe could not be so definitely determined. The word for pot resembles this, and it may mean a seething caldron.

After twenty minutes' sail from Kalai, Livingstone came in sight of five vast columns of vapor,
bending with the wind, and rising till their tops
mingled with the clouds. They were white toward the base, but dark further up, so as very
closely to resemble "smoke." The phenomenon
is just like that seen where large tracts of grass
are burning in Africa. The whole scene was
one of extraordinary beauty. The islands and
banks of the river are ornamented with trees of
great variety of color and form—some of them
covered with blossoms. "There, towering over
all, stands the great, burly baobab, each of whose
enormous arms would form the trunk of a large
tree, beside groups of graceful palms, which, with
their feathery-shaped leaves depicted on the sky,
lend their beauty to the scene. As a hiero-
glyphic, they always mean 'far from home,' for
one can never get over their foreign air in a
picture or a landscape. The silvery mohono,
which, in the tropics, is, in form, like the cedar
of Lebanon, stands in pleasing contrast with the
dark color of the motsouri, whose cypress-form
is dotted over at present with its pleasant, scarlet
fruit. Some trees resemble the great, spreading
oak; others assume the character of our own
elms and chestnuts; but no one can imagine the
beauty of the view from any thing witnessed in

England. It never had been seen before by European eyes ; but scenes so lovely must have been gazed upon by angels in their flight. The only want felt is that of mountains in the background."

On three sides of the falls there are ridges three or four hundred feet high, clothed with forest — the red soil to be seen occasionally among the trees. There is an island in the middle of the river at the falls, and right on the edge of the rock, over which the waters leap. In reaching this island there is danger of being swept down by the rapid currents rushing along either side. But, taking men well acquainted with the rapids, and a very light canoe, Livingstone landed upon the island in safety. Standing upon the island, within a few yards of the spot, the vast body of water seemed to disappear in the earth—the opposite lip of the fissure into which it fell being only eighty feet distant. Creeping with awe to the verge of the precipice, Livingstone peered down into the fearful chasm and saw a large crack or vent in the rock, reaching from bank to bank of the river, so that a stream of water a thousand yards wide leaped down a hundred feet, and, at the bottom of the falls, was suddenly compressed into the narrow compass of twenty yards. This narrow passage continues for miles through the basaltic rock of the hills, through which the waters roar, and rush, and boil. Our traveler pronounces this the most wonderful scene he witnessed in Africa. Looking down into the fissure, on the right of the island, he saw a dense white cloud, with two bright rainbows resting on it. From this cloud a jet of vapor rushed up, to the hight of two hundred or three hundred feet, looking just like steam. Reaching that hight, its hue was changed to that of dark smoke, and condensing there it fell back in a constant shower, which soon drenched the traveler thoroughly. This shower falls mainly on the opposite bank of the fissure. And à few yards back from its edge there stands a straight hedge of evergreen trees, whose leaves are always wet. From the roots of these trees a number of little rills run down the steep wall of rock into the gulf; but the column of vapor licks them entirely up, and bears them upward to the sky again. So though they are perpetually running down, they never reach the bottom of the gulf. The columns of vapor which have been spoken of are undoubtedly caused by the sudden compression of the water, falling from so great a hight into a wedge-shaped rocky basin. From measurement of the river at another point, Livingstone estimated the width immediately above the falls at a thousand yards. It was very low at the time of his visit, and he thought the width of water on the edge of the precipice was six hundred yards wide and three feet deep. The Makololo say the fissure through which the stream flows, below the falls, is deeper as you go eastward. There is one part of the wall where persons accustomed to it can go down by crouching to a sitting posture. The Makololo say they once pursued some Batoka people who, in the hurry of their flight, being unable to stop at the edge of the precipice, were dashed to pieces at the bottom. They saw the stream so far below that it looked like a "white cord." The depth of the abyss was so great—three hundred feet, probably—that they were glad to crawl away, "holding on to the ground."

On returning to Kalai, Livingstone told Sekeletu he had nothing else in his country worth showing, after the falls. This excited his curiosity to visit them the next day.

On the 20th of November the missionary bade farewell to Sekeletu, and pushed forward on his arduous journey, accompanied with one hundred and fourteen men whom Sekeletu furnished him to carry the ivory to the coast. The Batoka tribes who inhabit the islands and region of the Zambesi are very dark in color, while those living on the high lands are much lighter, or about the color of coffee and milk. They all follow the singular custom of knocking out the upper front teeth of both sexes at the age of maturity. Sebituane tried to eradicate the practice from those tribes under his authority, by inflicting severe punishment upon those parents who continued the custom with their children. But still the practice was kept up. When questioned respecting the origin of the practice, the Batoka say they do it to be like oxen. Those who retain their teeth they say are like zebras. The Makololo give a more laughable explanation. They say that the wife of a chief having bitten her husband, in a quarrel, he punished her by ordering her front teeth knocked out, and all the men in the tribe followed his example, with their wives. But this, of course, does not explain why they knocked out their own teeth too, as well as those of the women. A large number of these Batoka were in Livingstone's party.

For fear that the buffaloes in the country through which they were now passing had introduced tsetse, the oxen were moved only in the night, while Livingstone, with some of his attendants, marched on foot in the day-time. The company was divided into different parties or messes, each one having its head man, through whom orders were given from the white chief, and food distributed. Each party knew its own place in the encampment, and they took turns in pulling grass for Livingstone's bed.

The boabab-tree and a kind of sterculia, which is the most common tree in Loanda, flourish in this region. The moshuka-tree was bearing fruit at this time. The fruit tastes like a pear, and resembles in appearance a small apple. It has a harsh rind, and four large seeds. The tree grows to the hight of fifteen or twenty feet, and has large glossy leaves, as large as a man's hand. The men lived upon the fruit almost entirely for several days. The supply of rain had been small, the soil was quite dry, and the leaves drooped for want of moisture. But drought does not affect the fruit trees, unless it occurs at the time of their blossoming.

Abundance of maneko, a curious fruit, with a horny rind split in five pieces, was found. These sections, when chewed, are full of a glutinous matter—sweet as sugar. The fruit is about the size of the walnut, and the seeds—which are not eaten—are covered with a fine silky down. The Batoka ate the nju, a sort of bean, growing in a large square pod. They ate, too, the pulp between the seeds of the nux vomica and the motsintsela. The motsikiri is a magnificent tree which grows here, bearing dark evergreen leaves, and yielding oil. The Batoka say no one ever dies of hunger here, and the abundance of fruit leads one easily to credit the statement. A species of leucodendron which abounds here, when found where no rain has lately fallen, is seen to twist its leaves, during the heat of the day, so that only the edge is exposed to the sun. The acacias and mopanes, in similar circumstances, fold their leaves so as to present the smallest possible surface to the sun, like the eucalypti of Australia.

While stopping a day or two at the village of Marimba, Livingstone told these people, for the first time they had ever heard it, of the love of God shown in sending his Son to save them from sin and ruin.

While walking down to the forest one day, after addressing them, he saw many regiments of the black soldier-ants which he had frequently noticed in different parts of the country. They are so singular in their habits that a brief description of them will, doubtless, be interesting to the reader. They are about half an inch in length; black, with a tinge of gray. They march three or four abreast, and when disturbed utter a distinct hissing or chirping sound. They follow a few leaders, distinguished by their greater size,

and seem to be guided by a scent left on the
path by them.   If a handful of earth is thrown
on their path in the middle of a regiment, those
behind it are completely lost.   They come up to
the earth, but do not venture to cross it, though
not one-fourth of an inch in hight.   They wheel
around and regain their path; but never think of
retreating to their nest.   After fifteen minutes of
hissing and confusion, one of them will make a
circuit of a foot around the handful of earth, and,
striking the path beyond, the rest soon follow in
the same roundabout way.   A basin of water
thrown upon the path by which a regiment of
these curious insects had passed, puzzled them
for half an hour, when they came to it on their
return home.   The path was at last found, by one
bolder than the rest, making a long circuit around
the place where the water had fallen, and reaching the way beyond it.

They are in the habit of attacking the white
ants in their homes.   Soon as they are discovered
on the march by these latter species, they are
seen to rush about in the greatest fear and confusion.   The soldier-ants march upon them.   The
black leaders or captains seize the white ants, and
sting them, seeming to inject a fluid similar in
effect to chloroform, which renders their prey insensible, only having life enough to move one or

two front legs a little. The rank and file now seize them and carry them off.

It has been supposed by many who have studied the habits of these creatures, that they make slaves of the white ants; but Livingstone's observation shows that they never recover from the state of coma produced by the sting of the black leaders. Little heaps of the heads and legs of the white ants may be frequently found at the door where the black soldiers enter their barracks. Hence the evidence is pretty conclusive that these marauders are not slave-hunters, as they have been called, but cannibals. Livingstone saw a colony of them removing their eggs from a place where they were exposed to being flooded by recent rains. They numbered about twelve hundred. The eggs were carried a little distance by one party, and laid down, when others took them up and carried them farther on. Every ant in the colony seemed to be hard at work, but there were no white slave-ants.

There is a membrane-winged insect whose habits resemble those of the mason-bee, called the "plasterer," which injects a fluid from its sting that causes stupefaction, just as has been remarked of the soldier-ants. This insect is about one inch and one-fourth in length, and jet black. It may be seen coming into the house, carrying

in its fore legs a little ball of soft plaster about
the size of a pea. When it has found a suitable
place, it constructs a cell about the length of its
body, making the walls quite thin, and plastering
them smooth inside, leaving an opening at one
end. Then it brings seven or eight caterpillars
or spiders, made insensible by the fluid from its
sting, and deposits them in its cell. Then one of
its own larvæ is housed here, which as it grows
finds plenty of good fresh food. The caterpillars
are in a state of coma, but being still alive, do
not putrefy or dry up as they would if dead.

On the river Kalomo our party of travelers met
with an elephant without tusks—a very rare thing
in Africa. Even this huge animal is inspired with
fear of man, and this one moved off soon as she
discovered our party. Large herds of buffaloes
were here seen feeding in every direction. Crawl-
ing up close to a herd, Livingstone shot a fine
large one. The rest of the herd not seeing the
enemy gazed about in wonder, and then came
back to their wounded companion. It is the
habit of all these wild animals to gore a wounded
or sick companion, and expel him from the herd.
In this case the rest of the herd commenced an
attack upon the fallen buffalo, and when our
party of travelers made their appearance, continuing the goring while running away, they

lifted the wounded animal on their horns, and half supporting him in the crowd, bore him away. The scene afforded amusement to Livingstone's men, who thought the buffaloes were helping away their unfortunate comrade. He was shot between the fourth and fifth rib. The bullet passed through both lungs, and a rib on the opposite side—lodging against the skin. It was an eight-ounce ball, yet he ran some distance, and was killed by the spears of the men, who drove him into a pool of water, and there dispatched him.

The herd, which at first ran off in the direction of the camp, soon came bounding back again. Our travelers took refuge on an ant hill, and as they went past on full gallop, Livingstone had opportunity to observe that the leader of a herd of sixty was an old cow. She was allowed a full half length in front. On her withers about twenty buffalo birds were sitting. These birds are the guardian angels of the buffalo. When the animal is quietly feeding, the bird is seen hopping on the ground, picking up food, or sitting on the buffalo's back ridding it of the insects that sometimes burrow in its skin. The sight of the bird is more acute than that of the buffalo, and upon the approach of danger flies up, and thus gives warning to the animal, which immediately raises its head, and looks about to discover the danger. Sometimes the birds accompany the buffalo upon the wing in his flight, and at others ride upon his back.

Another bird, the *Buphaga Africanus*, attends the rhinoceros in a similar way. The Bechuanas call it "kala." When they wish to express their dependence upon another, they address him as "my rhinoceros," as if they were the birds.

The leader of a herd of animals is usually the most wary of all. That seems to be the principle upon which they are selected. When the herd sees any one of their number, or any other animal taking to flight, they invariably follow the example. Thus it is the most timid naturally becomes the leader. When a "leader" is shot, the whole herd are so bewildered that for a brief time they stop, and seem unable to decide which way to run. When the females bring forth their young, their shyness is very greatly increased. This seems to lead to what is so often witnessed among many of these animals—the division of the sexes into separate herds. This is annually seen among the antelopes. And the male and female elephants are never seen in one herd.

Sunday, the 10th of December, was spent at the village of Monze, who is chief of all the Batoka of this country. His town is near a hill,

called Kisekise. From this hill there is an extensive view of the country for a distance of thirty
miles around. The land is undulating, and open,
with but few trees. The people live in small villages—widely scattered. They cultivate large
gardens; but, though their country affords good
pasturage, they have no cattle—only a few goats
and fowls. Monze came to visit the "white
chief," on Sunday morning. He was wrapped in
a large cloth. He rolled himself over in the dust,
as an expression of homage to Livingstone, at
the same time screaming, "Kina bomba!" One
of his wives, who accompanied him, joined lustily
in the screaming, and was greatly excited—having never seen a white man before. She had a
small battle-ax in her hand, and would have
been comely in her looks if her teeth had been
spared. The chief Monze soon became quite
cordial and frank—spending most of the day in
conversation. He gave Livingstone a goat and
a fowl, and was highly pleased with a present of
handkerchiefs of printed cotton made him in return. The missionary placed a very gaudy handkerchief around the shoulders of Monze's child,
in the form of a shawl, which awakened so much
admiration that he said he would send for all his
people to come and dance around it.

One head man of a village after another

arrived, bringing the white man liberal supplies
of maize, ground-nuts, and corn. The same hospitality had, too, been shown all along at the villages by which the party had passed. In conversation with Monze and about one hundred and
fifty of his men, Livingstone told them his object
in journeying through their country was to open
up a path for the merchandise of ivory, so they
might avoid the guilt of selling their children.
He asked them if they would like to have a white
man live among them, and teach them. They
expressed the highest satisfaction with the propo-
sition, and promised to protect the white man
and his property. Livingstone desired to know
their feeling upon this question, because in any
attempt to civilize and teach the people of this
country it would be of the highest importance to
have stations in this healthy region, where missionaries might retire at times from .the more
sickly districts. It would be important, too, to
form a chain of communications in this way between the coast and the interior. These people
have no special desire for Christian instruction,
because they have no distinct idea of what it is.
But they would gladly welcome the residence of
white men among them, and they seem in a favorable condition to receive the Gospel.

The men of one village who came to the

encampment of the travelers wore their hair after
the Bashukulompo fashion. A circle of hair on
the top of the head, eight inches in diameter at
the base, is woven something like basket-work,
into a cone eight or ten inches high, with an obtuse apex, bent a little forward in some instances,
so as to give it the appearance of a helmet. The
head man of the village, instead of having his
brought to a point, had it prolonged into a wand,
a yard long. Monze said this was the fashion
among all his people; but he discouraged it.
Livingstone desired him to discourage the practice of knocking out the teeth; but he thought
fashion was too strong for his authority in that
case. At their departure, on Monday, Monze
presented the travelers with a piece of buffalo,
which had been killed the day before by lions.

Our party now moved northward across the
rivulet Makoe, to visit Semalembue, a chief of
influence residing there. The villagers still supplied them with abundance of food. In passing
through some woods upon this trip, Livingstone
for the first time heard the cry of the bird called
by the natives "Mokwa reza," or son-in-law of
God. The natives say its cry is "Pula, pula"—
rain, rain. They say it is heard only just before
the fall of heavy rains. It is said to throw the
eggs of the white-backed Sengal crow out of

their nest, and lay its own instead. For this reason, and its cry for rain, this bird is a favorite
among these people. The crow, on the other
hand, has a bad reputation, and when there is a
dearth of rain the people seek its nest, and destroy its eggs, to dissolve the charm, by which it
is thought to have shut up the windows of heaven.
From its habits, Livingstone suggests that the
mokwa reza may be a cuckoo.

The country through which we are now passing, as we follow the footsteps of the great
missionary, is very beautiful, and furrowed with
deep valleys. In one of these valleys—a fine
green one, studded here and there with trees,
and cut with rivulets—Livingstone found a buffalo lying down, and attempted to kill him for
food. But he would not die easily. After receiv-
ing three shots, he turned round to charge his
enemy, and Livingstone ran for shelter toward
some rocks in the distance; but before he reached
them, he found his retreat cut off by three elephants, who had been attracted to the scene by
the unusual noise. In a moment or two, however, they turned short off, and gave him a chance
to reach the rocks. Looking out from his place
of refuge, he saw the buffalo running away quite
briskly. Not relishing the thought of complete
disappointment in the supply of meat, he tried a

long shot at the hindmost of the elephants, and, to the great joy of the men, broke his fore leg. The young men now cut off his retreat, and brought him to a stand, when a shot in the head dispatched him. This abundant supply of meat was received with demonstrations of joy, and many people from the villages near by came to participate in the feast.

Having retired from the noise to take an observation among some rocks, Livingstone on the next day saw an elephant and her calf at the end of the valley, about two miles away. The calf was finding pleasure in rolling in the mud, while its mother was standing quietly by, fanning herself with her great ears. Looking at them through his glass, Livingstone saw a company of his men making their appearance on the other side of them. His man Sekwebu had told him the men went off that morning saying, "Our father will see to-day what sort of men he has got." Livingstone now went higher up the side of the hill, to get a better view of their method of hunting. The young elephant seemed about two years old. Its dam was a goodly beast. Unconscious of approaching danger, they both went into a pit of mud, and smeared themselves all over. Then the calf, after having been suckled, frisked and played about its mother, flapping his

ears, and tossing his trunk. The mother mean-
time gave expression of enjoyment, by flapping
her ears, and wagging her tail. Suddenly the
men began blowing through a tube, making the
piping noise which boys sometimes do by blowing in a key or between the hands. Both beasts
expanded their ears and listened, and, as the
crowd rushed toward them, left their bath in
haste. The young one ran toward the end of
the valley; but seeing the men there, returned to
his mother. She placed herself between the
enemy and her calf, running sidewise for a part
of the time. The men kept up a ceaseless piping and shouting, and followed her at a distance
of about a hundred yards. When she came to
cross a rivulet, the time spent in descending one
bank and climbing the opposite permitted their
coming up to the edge, and within twenty yards
of their game, so as to throw their spears into
her. Her sides were soon red with blood, and
•she began to flee for her life, seeming to forget
her young. She sometimes turned and made a
charge at her pursuers; but they dodged away at
right-angles, and she went straight on, passing
through the whole party without harming any
one. But being constantly attacked with fresh
spears, she was at last killed by loss of blood.
Sekwebu had been sent by Livingstone with

orders to spare the calf; but before he reached the men they had killed him.

The elephant killed by Livingstone was a male, not full grown. Its hight at the withers was eight feet and four inches. The circumference of the fore foot was seven feet four inches. The female killed by the men was full grown, and measured in hight eight feet and eight inches; circumference of the fore foot, eight feet. Her ear was four feet five inches in depth, and four feet in horizontal breadth. No attempt has been made in modern times to tame the African elephant; but inscriptions upon ancient coins show they were domesticated and found very docile and tractable by the Romans.

Leaving the elephant valley, and passing the rivulet Losito, the travelers came to the village of Semalembue. This chief visited them soon after their arrival, and presented them five or six baskets of meal and maize, and a huge one of ground-nuts; and on the next morning he brought them twenty baskets more of meal. Livingstone had but little to give him in return; but he accepted very politely the apologies which were offered. He expressed great joy at the Gospel promise of peace, of which the missionary spoke. This chief obtains ivory from surrounding tribes, on pretense of possessing some supernatural power. He exchanges this ivory with other chiefs on the Zambesi for cotton goods, which come from Mozambique by Babisa traders.

Semalembue accompanied our party upon their departure to the ford of the Rafue River. On parting with him, Livingstone gave him a shirt, with which he was highly pleased. The supply of meat having run low, Livingstone shot a hippopotamus—a full-grown cow. Its flesh is much like pork. This animal measured four feet and ten inches in hight, and ten feet six inches from the point of the nose to the root of the tail.

As our travelers neared the river Zambesi, they found the country thickly covered with broad-leaved bushes. At an open space a herd of buffaloes came trotting up to look at the oxen. They were taught the propriety of retreating only when one of their number was shot. Elephants had often to be driven out of the path by loud shouting. One day a female elephant, with three young ones, came charging through the center of the caravan, making the men throw down their burdens in very great haste. For her temerity she received a spear. The river was reached about eight miles east of its confluence with the Rafue. The Zambesi is much wider here than above the falls, at Sesheke. One

might try in vain to make his voice heard across
it. Its current is more rapid here, being often
four and a half miles an hour, and the water is of
a deep brownish red.

Traveling along the banks of the Zambesi for
many days, our party were for the most part
treated very kindly by the villagers. In one or
two instances, their objects being misunderstood,
they were threatened with attacks by different
chiefs ; but succeeded in pacifying them, so as to
avoid all bloodshed.

On one occasion, soon after having passed the
confluence of the Loangwa and Zambesi, while
moving among the trees, where the underbrush
was very dense and high, three buffaloes, who
thought they were surrounded by the men, dashed
through their line. Livingstone's ox started off
upon the gallop, and when he managed to look
back he saw one of the men in the air about five
feet above a buffalo. Coming back, he found the
poor fellow had lighted on his face, and, though
carried for twenty yards on the horns of the buffalo before getting the final toss, he had not a
bone broken or a fracture in his skin. He had
thrown down his burden at the appearance of the
buffalo, and stabbed him in the side. The beast
turned suddenly upon him, and bore him away
before he could take refuge in a tree. His

comrades shampooned him well, and in a week
he was able to engage in the hunt again.

On the 2d of March the travel-worn missionary
camped about eight miles from the Portuguese
town of Tete, or Nyungwe. The men wished to
go on, but Livingstone, being very much fatigued,
lay down to rest, and sent a messenger forward
with letters of introduction to the comnfandant,
with which he had been favored by the Bishop
of Angola and others. About two o'clock next
morning he was awakened by two officers and a
company of soldiers, who had been sent to escort
him to the town. They brought the materials
for a civilized breakfast. The food of the party
had been exhausted, and long absence from all
the comforts and marks of civilization had prepared Livingstone to appreciate such a meal. It
cured his fatigue, though he had been so tired
the night before that he could not sleep. He
says: "It was the most refreshing breakfast I
ever partook of, and I walked the last eight miles
without the least feeling of weariness, although
the path was so rough that one of the officers
remarked to me, 'This is enough to tear a man's
life out of him.'"

Arriving at Tete, he was received with much
kindness by the commandant, Tito Augusto
d'Araujo Sicard. He gave the men abundant

provisions of millet, and provided them lodgings till they could erect huts for themselves. By this means they were protected from the bite of the tampans, here called carapators—an insect whose bite is quite dangerous—sometimes causing fatal fever. "It may please our homeopathic friends to hear that in curing the bite of the tampan the natives administer one of the insects bruised in the medicine employed." Major Sicard urged Livingstone to remain with him till the following month, as the sickly season at Kilimane was not yet over.

The village of Tete is built on the sloping bank of the river Zambesi. The strata of the gray sandstone beneath it have a crumpled form. The houses are built on the elevated fold of the rock, and each depression or crease forms the street. There are about thirty European houses, built of stone, and cemented with mud instead of lime. They are thatched with reeds and grass. The mud having been washed out from between the stones by the rains, the houses have a rough, untidy look. Besides these, there are about twelve hundred huts, in which the natives live. The population may be about four thousand, a part of whom are absent a considerable portion of the time, engaged in agricultural operations in the adjoining country. Gold dust is found in this vicinity. Some fine seams of coal were seen by Livingstone, and iron of a superior quality is abundant. Our traveler visited a hot spring, a little way up the river from Tete, the water of which has a temperature of 160°, and is too hot for the hand, where it flows over the stones.

While at Tete, Livingstone inquired of Major Sicard if any plant was known in the country from which paper might be manufactured, and in response to the inquiry the Major showed him specimens of the fibrous tissue of a species of aloe, called conge, and of a plant called Bwaze, and also fibers from the root of a wild date. These fibers were sent to Messrs. Pye Brothers, of London, who, after experimenting with them, gave a favorable opinion of the Bwaze as a substitute for flax, though, probably, not of much value for paper.

Livingstone also found while here a very excellent substitute for quinine, in the root bark of a tree called kumbanzo, which the natives use as a remedy for fever. The Portuguese use the bark of the tree. The flowers are said to be white. It bears pods in pairs, a foot or fifteen inches in length. Several other plants are employed by the natives in the treatment of fever.

Having waited here a month, for the beginning of the healthy season at Killimane, Livingstone

wished to start for that place on the 1st of April;
but waited a few days for the appearance of the
moon, in order to take lunar observations on his
way down the river. On the fourth day, however, a new cause of delay occurred. A sudden change of temperature, at the time of the
moon's appearance, gave the Doctor, Major Sicard, and nearly every person in the house, a severe fever. Dr. Livingstone, however, soon cured
himself and the hospitable friends whose kindness he had shared, and on the 22d he left Tete,
for a canoe journey down the Zambesi, attended
by Lieutenant Miranda, an escort sent by Commandant Sicard, and sixteen of his own men.
The Commandant continued his generous hospitality by abundant provisions for the journey.
He sent letters to his friends along the river asking them to treat Livingstone as they would
himself. He gave orders to Lieutenant Miranda
not to permit his guest to pay for any thing in
the whole journey to the coast. Livingstone
speaks in the highest terms of Portuguese hospitality.

A sail of five days down the magnificent Zambesi brought him to Senna. This voyage was
made in a canoe, paddled by two men, a shed
over a part of it being provided for Livingstone.
A few days after leaving Senna he was violently

attacked with tertian fever. "The pulse beat with amazing force and felt as if thumping against the crown of the head."

Fortunately he fell in with Senhor Asevedo, at Interra, of whose reputation for kindness and generosity all who ever visited Killimane have heard. He had a large sail-boat, with a house in the stern, which he at once offered for Livingstone's accommodation. This added greatly to the comfort of the sick and exhausted traveler, and on the 20th of May, 1856, he reached the village of Killimane, on the western coast of Africa. It wanted only a few days of four years since he made his departure from Cape Town upon this long, perilous, and toilsome journey over a wild, uncultivated country, in a hot climate, and among savage men. And all this toil and hardship, endured so heroically, was undertaken, not for personal gain, or love of adventure, or advantage of any kind, but from a benevolent desire to elevate and Christianize the barbarous and untaught tribes of Africa. But let the hero-missionary speak for himself:

"As far as I am myself concerned, the opening of the new central country is a matter of congratulation only in so far as it opens up a prospect for the elevation of the inhabitants. I view the end of the geographical feat as the beginning of the missionary enterprise. I take the latter term in its most extended signification, and include every effort made for the amelioration of our race, the promotion of all those means by which God in his providence is working and bringing all his dealings with man to a glorious consummation. Each man in his sphere, either knowingly or unwittingly, is performing the will of our Father in heaven. Men of science searching after hidden truths, which, when discovered, will, like the electric telegraph, bind men more closely together—soldiers battling for the right against tyranny—sailors rescuing the victims of oppression from the grasp of heartless men-stealers—merchants teaching the nations lessons of mutual dependence—and many others as well as missionaries, all work in the same direction, and all efforts are overruled for one glorious end.

"If the reader has accompanied me thus far, he may, perhaps, be disposed to take an interest in the objects I propose to myself, should God mercifully grant me the honor of doing something more for Africa. As the highlands on the borders of the central basin are comparatively healthy, the first object seems to be to secure a permanent path thither, in order that Europeans may pass quickly as possible through the unhealthy region near the coast. The river has

not been surveyed, but at the time I came down
there was abundance of water for a large vessel,
and this continues through four or five months
of each year. . . . When we get beyond the
hostile population"—near the coast—"we reach a
very different race. On the latter my chief hopes
at present rest. All of them, however, are willing and anxious to engage in trade, and, while
eager for this, none of them have ever been encouraged to cultivate the raw materials of commerce. Their country is well adapted for cotton.
. . . We ought to encourage the Africans to
cultivate for our markets, as the most effectual
means, next to the Gospel, of their elevation.

"It is in the hope of working out this idea that
I propose the formation of stations on the Zambesi beyond the Portuguese territory, but having
communication through them with the coast. A
chain of stations admitting of easy and speedy
intercourse, such as might be formed along the
flank of the eastern ridge, would be in favorable
position for carrying out the objects in view.
The London Missionary Society has resolved to
have a station among the Makololo on the north
bank, and another on the south bank among the
Matabele. The Church—Wesleyan, Baptist, and
that most energetic body, the Free Church—
could each find desirable locations among the

Batoka and adjacent tribes. The country is so extensive, there is no fear of clashing. All classes of Christians find that sectarian rancor dies out when they are working for the real heathen."

Livingstone left his friends at Kilimane on the 12th of July, taking Sekwebu with him. As they rode out to the brig "Frolic," on which they were to sail for England, the waves were high, and often swept over the boat. Sekwebu was much frightened, as these fearful waves came dashing over them, and said to Livingstone, "Is this the way you go? Is this the way you go?" "Yes, don't you see it is," said Livingstone smiling, and then he tried to encourage him. He was well acquainted with canoes, but had never seen any thing like this.

On the 12th of August they reached the Mauritius, and were towed into the harbor by a steamer. Sekwebu became a great favorite with the officers and men on board the brig. Every thing was so strange to him on a man-of-war that he seemed bewildered, and at last the constant excitement produced insanity. He went down the side of the brig into a boat, and when Livingstone attempted to go down to bring him up he ran to the stern, and said "No! no! it is enough that I die alone. You must not perish.

If you come, I shall throw myself into the water." Observing that he was not in his right mind, Livingstone said to him, " Now, Sekwebu, we are going to ma-Robert." This touched a tender chord in his bosom, and, seeming to recover his reason, he said, "O, yes! where is she? and where is Robert?"

The officers of the brig proposed to secure him, by putting him in irons; but Livingstone refused his consent, knowing that the insane often remember the ill-treatment they have received after recovery; and as Sekwebu was a gentleman in his own country, Livingstone could not think of having it reported there that he had put one of Sekeletu's principal men in chains, as only slaves were treated in that country.

He tried to get Sekwebu on shore during the day, but he refused to go, and in the evening a new paroxysm of insanity came on. He attempted to spear one of the crew, and then leaped overboard. He could swim well; but he pulled himself down by the chain-cable, hand over hand, and his body was never found. Making his voyage by the way of the Red Sea, Livingstone reached his loved native land, "Old England," on the 12th of December, A. D. 1856, after an absence of sixteen years, and a separation from his family of nearly five years.

Subsequently he returned to Africa, to continue his labors for the elevation and Christian instruction of her benighted tribes.

THE END.

www.ingramcontent.com/pod-product-compliance
Lightning Source LLC
Chambersburg PA
CBHW021218270326
41929CB00010B/1174